We're from Kelso

Kelso Connections

Publication Data

Published by
Friends of Kelso Museum
Maxwellheugh Cottage
Jedburgh Road
Kelso
TD5 8AZ

This edition edited by Ruth Holmes.

ISBN 978 0 9563397 1 3

Designed, typeset and printed by Kelso Graphics.

Kelso Connections gratefully acknowledge the generous contributions from the Kelso Laddies Association (Year of Homecoming grant) and Charity Begins at Home.

Front Cover photograph of Kelso by Hector Innes.
Front Cover Civic Week photograph by Alastair Watson, Southern Reporter.
Back Cover photograph – Kelso Connections Group – From Left to Right,
Isabel Gordon, Christine Henderson, Colin Henderson and Ruth Holmes.

Kelso has, certainly, played her part in "The Year of Homecoming", 2009. A year, throughout which, Scotland has, with typical hospitality, warmly welcomed those who have proudly returned to their Scottish roots. Towns and cities throughout the land have demonstrated pride in their communities, their culture and their heritage. Kelso has been no exception. The enthusiasm of our "Kelso Connections" group has ensured the success of Kelso's own celebration of her heritage and culture. The group enabled a variety of organisations to work together and to develop an interesting programme of community events, based upon the Scottish Borders' "Return to the Ridings" theme. The programme was launched in the spring, when it was first announced that our businesses and shops were willing to display a series of descriptive story boards. Each board would carry information relating to people of note, who had once lived in Kelso. The subsequent interest in the town centre exhibition certainly surpassed all expectations and has provided the inspiration for this eagerly awaited book.

Down through the centuries, talented Scots have distinguished themselves in; Arts and Humanities, Engineering and Invention, Medicine and the Sciences, the Armed Services, Sporting prowess, Discovery and Exploration. Scottish endeavour and accomplishment has, justifiably, received international acclaim. The "We're from Kelso" exhibition boards afforded us an opportunity to discover the laudable achievements of a collection of inspirational men and women, connected with our own town. What a fascinating glimpse we have

had into their lives. The diverse list of Kelso's people includes: an Olympic medallist, a celebrated Victorian novelist, young soldiers lost in the horrors of Gallipoli, New World adventurers and pioneers, a broadcaster and writer, an opera singer - so many distinguished people. Kelsonians and their visitors have been intrigued to learn about other Kelsonians - some of them, possibly their own contemporaries who, for a summer, have been joined (within the windows of our town centre) by figures from the past; people who, in bygone days, also walked the familiar cobbled streets of our bonnie Border town.

The Kelso Connections group had not, initially, set out with the intention of compiling their carefully researched information into a book. However the exhibition stimulated so much public interest that it quickly became clear that Kelso's people wished to have this information published and available to them. This demand has been satisfied, the story boards now form the interesting, illustrated pages within which our collection of remarkable people are permanently assembled. Throughout "The Year of Homecoming", Kelso Connections has successfully connected many people within our community, through a variety of enjoyable opportunities and events. The success of the storyboard project and the consequent compilation of this book are, primarily, due to the vision and enthusiastic commitment of Ruth Holmes, Christine Henderson, Isabel Gordon and Colin Henderson. To their credit we have, unexpectedly, gained a new book to add to our knowledge of Kelso's rich heritage. I am sure that it will be widely read and enjoyed.

Fiona S Scott
Honorary Provost of Kelso

Kelso Connections

For the Year of Homecoming 2009 Scottish Borders Council chose to promote the wealth of history celebrated by Civic Weeks and Common Ridings held throughout the Scottish Borders every summer.

Funding was provided by the Scottish Government to allow the local festivals to promote a community event through a project called "Return to the Ridings". The Kelso Laddies Association decided to base a project on the Colour Bussing which is a colourful event on the Wednesday evening of Civic Week when the Kelso Laddie is presented with the Kelso Standard and it is then bussed by 4 young Lady Bussers from the local primary schools.

The prologue to the Bussing Ceremony states, "In peacetime and wartime men from Kelso have gone out to the four corners of the world in pursuit of their duty, and we symbolise our recognition of their deeds by our Kelso Laddie dipping the Town Flag to the North, South, East and West of Kelso Square. At each of these points a Lady Busser will tie a Blue or White Ribbon to the Standard. These four Ribbons bear one word each, Freedom, Honour, Valour and Wisdom"

Expanding this to men and women from Kelso and surrounding villages it was developed further as a community project. Several local organisations came together to create Kelso Connections under the umbrella of Kelso Community Events. These organisations were Friends of Kelso Museum, Kelso Library, Kelso and District Amenity Society and Kelso Laddies Association. Kelso Connections as well as compiling the information for the "We're from Kelso" exhibition (which has subsequently been turned into this book) organised displays, talks and events to run through the Year of Homecoming. Further financial sponsorship came from the Kelso Laddies Association, the Ex Kelso Laddies and Charity Begins at Home.

The idea was to portray in colourful storyboards biographies of characters with Kelso connections who have made their mark throughout the world, the aim being to tell locals and tourists alike about the contribution people from Kelso have made through the ages.

The project attracted considerable attention. The storyboards were exhibited in the shops of Kelso from Kelso Civic Week in July until St James Fair in September. Tourists and locals alike were observed reading the boards and many entered the competition which ran for the length of the exhibition with questions based on the world wide geographical coverage of the storyboards. Prizes were donated by Kelsonian author Alistair Moffat who was himself the subject of one of the boards.

As well as organisations many individuals gave freely of their time to research and produce materials for which Kelso Connections are very grateful. A special mention must go to the staff of Kelso Graphics who not only supported the project but produced materials above and beyond the call of duty.

Kelso Laddies Association

In 1937, the combination of a Charities Parade, the Local Shopping week and the service for those who fell at Gallipoli resulted in the first Civic Week with a Kelso Laddie - Bobby Service.

The Kelso Laddie now leads an annual cavalcade to Yetholm to qualify for his Blue Bonnet for having crossed the English Border. The Historical Pageant of the Whipman's Ride re-enacts the sporting festivities of a very early trade union. Not every event is based on equestrian skills, a Grand Ball and a Children's Ball are mainstays of the week, and the War Memorial and joint church service, as well as the Fancy Dress Parade are still key elements of the week.

The highlight of the week is the Colour Bussing of the town flag in the beautifully decorated Town Square, in front of a large crowd, when the Kelso Laddie is still entrusted with the Burgh Standard. Kelso Civic Week takes place annually, normally during the third week of July.

It was funding from Scottish Borders Council to promote the Return to the Ridings, given to the Kelso Laddies Association, which was the catalyst for the "We're from Kelso" exhibition. The Kelso Laddies Association, a proud partner in Kelso Connections would like to thank all who have worked hard in partnership to provide such a worthwhile community project in the Year of the Homecoming 2009.

Colin Henderson
Master of Ceremonies

Kelso Library

Built in 1906 with a grant from Andrew Carnegie, Kelso Library is a popular community hub, and is the fourth busiest library in the Scottish Borders.

Kelso Library provides books, dvds, talking books, cds, free Internet access, community & tourist information, job point, newspapers, fax and photocopying facilities and lots more.

An active Friends of Kelso Library group supports the library with time, skills and energy. They host author visits, illustrated talks and poetry events. Kelso Library Readers Group meet regularly to discuss books, poetry and the world in general!

Youngsters are catered for with our Rhymetime sessions which are very popular with mums and tots and great fun. Local schools regularly visit the library for storytelling sessions and to discover the magical world of books.

Kelso Library Centenary Garden was opened in April 2007 and has given enjoyment to many of our readers. Funded by Awards for All, Charity Begins at Home, Abbey Row Community Centre, Friends of Kelso Library and Scottish Borders Council it has provided a unique addition to the library and a peaceful place to sit on warm days.

Kelso Library is open
Monday & Friday	10–1, 2–5
Tuesday & Thursday	10–1, 2–5, 5.30–7
Wednesday	10–1
Saturday	9.30 – 12.30

Ruth Holmes
Librarian

Kelso and District Amenity Society

Kelso and District Amenity Society exists to promote and encourage interest in and care for the beauty, history and character of the town of Kelso and its surrounding district. While our chief concern is with protecting the built heritage of the town, and more especially the buildings and character of the Conservation Area, our interest extends to anything to do with the condition of the town's public spaces and amenities. We meet every two months when, typically we discuss planning applications (we are regularly consulted by Scottish Borders Council on plans for the Conservation Area) plus a wide range of other matters, from major developments like supermarkets and traffic management schemes to litter bins and grass cutting problems. We are also responsible for the creation and maintaining of the Walter Scott Trail in Kelso.

Christine Henderson
Honorary Secretary

Friends of Kelso Museum

In 1981 the then Borders Regional Council created an award-winning Museum on the first floor of Turret House (one of the oldest houses in Kelso). At the same time, the Friends of Kelso Museum was formed to promote awareness of Kelso's historical importance and to support the work of the Museum. In 1996 the blow fell – the Museum would close at the end of the season. The usual reason – Council 'cuts'. The collection was put into store in the Town Hall (where it can still be accessed by request to Scottish Borders Council's Museum's Service).

The Friends of Kelso Museum still exists. The Museum had always been seasonal, so the Friend's main activity was arranging a series of public lectures during the closed winter months, on local history themes. This we have continued to do. We have also mounted a number of exhibitions in the Town Hall either by ourselves, or in conjunction with other local groups.

Isabel Gordon
Chairman

Acknowledgements

Kelso Connections would like to thank the following for the use of illustrations in this book:

Abbotsford House; Alistair Moffat; Arthur Hastie; Catherine Reid; Christine Henderson; Ednam House Hotel; Friends of Kelso Museum; Hector Innes; Heritage Hub, Hawick; John Robson; John Scott; Kelso and District Amenity Society; Kelso Archive Collection; Ken Nichol; Margaret Riddell; National Museums of Scotland; Portora Royal School, Enniskillen; Rosemary Payne; Scottish Borders Sporting Hall of Fame; SCRAN; Sir Matthew Pinsent; Sir William Purves; Southend-on-Sea Borough Council; Stephen Luscombe; Thora Ker; Southern Reporter and University of Edinburgh Fine Art Collection.

Grateful thanks to the following for their support and research:

Ian Abernethy; Susanne Batchelor, SBC Cultural Coordinator; Lady Mary Biddulph; John Crombie; Helen Darling; Charlie Denoon; Oliver Drake; David Ferguson; Arthur Hastie; Heritage Hub, Hawick; Alasdair Hutton; Kelso Community Events; Kelso Graphics; Alex McCue; The late Audrey Mitchell; Margaret Riddell; John Scott and Bill Smith.

Thanks also to the following shops for displaying the boards:

All Pets; Bannerman Burke; Blairs; Browns; Card Shop; Carpet Shop; Charity Begins at Home; Collins Fish Shop; Countryside Cookware; Darling Buds of Kelso; Forrest of Kelso; Hawick Cashmere; Hector Innes; Honor Murray Antiques; Horseshoe Gallery; Hume Painter; Inspirations; Itzy Bitzy; Jay & Jay; Jeffrey James; Kelso Travel; Kelso Wholefoods; Latimer Books; Liba; Little Feet of Kelso; McColl; McNab Saddlers; Nature's Way; Orvis; Pams Flower Box; Pride & Joy; Scottish Borders Council Registrars; Seasons Coffee Shop; Snipz 'n' clipz; Stewart & Son; Swans; Threshers; Tweedside Tackle; Visit Scotland Information Centre.

Charity Begins at Home window display during the "We're from Kelso" Exhibition.

The Horseshoe Gallery window display during the "We're from Kelso" Exhibition.

Contents

James Ballantyne

1770-1833

James Ballantyne
Courtesy of Abbotsford House

James Ballantyne was the son and grandson of successful Kelso merchants who ran a business at the corner of the Square. He attended Kelso Grammar School, and it was there in 1783 that he first made friends with Walter Scott who was his fellow-pupil for several months, while Scott stayed with his aunt in Kelso. James went on to study Law at Edinburgh University, then returned to Kelso to practice as a solicitor in 1795.

He was soon involved in a new venture, the *Kelso Mail* newspaper, which first appeared on April 13th 1797. After a chance meeting with Scott, Ballantyne invited him to write a legal article for his newspaper. When Scott visited Ballantyne's printing office in Bridge Street, he suggested that James should try some book printing work as well as newspapers. As a result of this conversation, Ballantyne printed first a limited edition of a few of Scott's ballads *Apology for Tales of Terror*, and then in 1802 a much larger work, *The Minstrelsy of the Scottish Border*. This was a great success and soon ran into a second edition.

Walton Hall

By 1803 Ballantyne had been persuaded to move his business to Edinburgh. *The Minstrelsy* was soon followed by *The Lay of the Last Minstrel, Marmion* and other best sellers. In 1811, with *Waverley*, published anonymously, Scott launched into his career as the best selling novelist of his day. He had also by this time become a major partner in Ballantyne's printing business, providing it with the capital to expand.

At the end of 1825 the partners were struck with disaster. Following a collapse in the publishing business which ruined Scott's publisher Constable, it was discovered that the Ballantyne printing company was seriously in debt. Faced with ruin, Scott stood by his friend Ballantyne, admitted publicly his role in the business, and undertook to pay off the debts from the proceeds of his writing. Their affairs were put in charge of a trust and Ballantyne was allowed to continue as manager of the business.

Minstrelsy of the Scottish Border

The huge success of Scott as a novelist owed much to Ballantyne who not only printed all his works but also proof read and corrected them, and often offered his advice on matters of style and language. Ballantyne died in March 1833, just a few months after his life-long friend Walter Scott.

The Other Ballantynes

John Ballantyne James's brother was for several years Scott's agent and publisher, and copied out his manuscripts, to preserve the secret of the author's identity. He built Walton Hall in Roxburgh Street, but died before it was finished.

Alexander Ballantyne the youngest brother ran the *Kelso Mail* after James went to Edinburgh. He lived briefly in Walton Hall then moved to Edinburgh to help in the business. His son **R. M. Ballantyne** was a best selling children's author.

Horatius Bonar was descended from a long line of Church of Scotland Ministers. After Edinburgh University, he became a "missionary assistant" in Leith. He quickly realised that the Sunday School children could not relate to the psalms – at that time the only singing allowed in church – and started writing poems they could understand and enjoy, setting them to popular tunes of the day. From this beginning he would go on to write over 600 hymns.

Bonar was called to be the first minister of the newly built North Church in Inch Road, Kelso, being inducted and ordained on the day it was opened, 26th November 1837. Six years later came 'The Disruption' which was to tear the Church of Scotland apart. At the General Assembly in Edinburgh on 18th May 1843, Rev. David Welsh read a protest against interference in a congregation's right to choose a minister. He walked out, followed by an impromptu procession of elders and ministers. Out of the 1200 clergy, some 450 seceded, including Horatius Bonar with his entire congregation. For many ministers, it meant losing their house and stipend and for their congregation its place of worship. In Kelso, it merely meant changing the name to Kelso North Free Church and it was to be 19 years before the Church of Scotland claimed back the building, precipitating the move to Roxburgh Street.

As well as hymns, Bonar was to make a name for himself as the author of the KELSO TRACTS which set out in a clear, simple way, the Gospel message. It is said that his tract of 1839 Believe and Live was loved by Queen Victoria, who regularly gave it to people. Others such as God's Way of Holiness and God's Way of Peace sold in their thousands and were translated into French, German and Gaelic. Bonar wrote a number of books and was for many years editor of 'The Border Watch' and 'The Quarterly Journal of Prophecy'. He firmly believed that Christ's return was imminent. Bonar conducted meetings in farm kitchens, village schools and the open air, speaking in a way that even the simplest folk could understand. In 1855, in need

of a break, he journeyed to the Holy Land. Many of his hymns from this trip were written on the back of a camel! Some of the best loved are Thy way, not mine, O Lord; the communion hymn Here, O my Lord, I see thee face to face and the uplifting Glory be to God the Father.

In 1866 Bonar left Kelso to become minister of the new Chalmers Memorial Free Church at Grange in Edinburgh. He was elected Moderator of the General Assembly of the Free Church in 1883 and celebrated the jubilee of his ministry in 1888, dying in 1889 after a long illness.

Kelso North Parish Church

In 1843, Horatius Bonar married Jane Lundie, third daughter of the Rev. Robert Lundie, Minister of Kelso Parish Church and sister of Mary Lundie. Jane like her husband and sister also wrote hymns, but none became well known.

Mary Lundie Duncan 1814-1840

Mary's grandfather Cornelius Lundie was minister at Kelso 1750-1800 and her father, Robert returned there as minister in 1807. Mary was taught with her brothers, learning Latin. Later, at boarding school in London she heard Wilberforce and others speak about the emancipation of slaves. She returned to Kelso in 1832, during a cholera epidemic, shortly before her father's sudden death, after which the family had to quit the manse for Edinburgh. There Mary became a school visitor, helping pupils' families and regularly visited women in the workhouse.

In 1836, Mary married W. Wallace Duncan, son of her father's greatest friends Dr. Henry Duncan of Ruthwell, Dr. Henry Duncan was a founder of the Trustees Savings Bank and its first branch opened at Ruthwell. This probably influenced Mary's father Rev. Robert Lundie to set up the "Kelso Friendly Bank Society" around 1815. Once an investor saved more than £10, he was expected to transfer his account to the Bank of Scotland.

Mary had a daughter and a son and continued to teach and take an interest in the welfare of servant girls. Like her brother-in-law Horatius Bonar, she began to write simple poems and hymns, the most loved of which is Jesus, tender shepherd, hear me. She died after catching a chill, aged just 25.

Sir Thomas Makdougall Brisbane

1773-1860

Portrait of General Sir Thomas Brisbane c. 1840, by Robert Frain

Born in Brisbane House, Largs, in 1773, Thomas Brisbane began his military career at the age of 15, seeing service with the Duke of Wellington in Ireland and subsequently in Flanders, the West Indies, the Peninsula and Canada. He was twice wounded, decorated for his services in the Peninsula, appointed KCB and reached the rank of Major-General. In 1816 he saved the Paris Observatory from destruction by allied troops and was created a Knight of the Cross of Hanover.

In 1819, at the age of 46, he married Anna Maria, the daughter and heiress of Sir Henry Hay-Makdougall of Makerstoun, Kelso and added her name to his. They were to have four children, all of whom predeceased their parents. In 1821, on the recommendation of the Iron Duke, Brisbane was appointed fifth Governor of New South Wales and Van Diemen's Land (now Tasmania) succeeding Governor Macquarie.

New South Wales principally comprised the penal settlement of Botany Bay, but Brisbane promoted voluntary free immigration to the colony. He encouraged the planting of grape-vines, sugar cane, tea and tobacco plants as well as the rearing of sheep and cattle and pure-bred Arabian horses. He also licensed a free press. In 1822 he established an astronomical observatory at Parramatta, Sydney. Until then, the southern hemisphere skies were virtually uncharted. Brisbane sponsored exploration towards what is today known as Queensland and John Oxley, in exploring northwards from Sydney along the coast, discovered a river which he named Brisbane, on which the eponymous capital of Queensland came to be built. In 2003 the city erected a memorial plaque and seat to Sir Thomas Brisbane.

He was recalled to Britain on 1st December 1825. Thereafter, he concentrated on astronomy and geophysics at Makerstoun and Largs. In 1832 Brisbane was elected President of the Royal Society in Edinburgh, in succession to Sir Walter Scott. In 1836 Sir Thomas was created a Baronet of the UK by King William IV and a KGCB, being further appointed GCB in 1837. To present it, William IV invited him to dine at the Palace 'next Wednesday'. Alas, the King died on Tuesday, 20th June 1837.

At Makerstoun in 1841, Brisbane began important magnetic observations through which he discovered magnetic north and erected north and south meridian stones either side of the Tweed.

Drawing of Makerstoun observatories from Transactions 1844 of the Royal Society of Edinburgh

MILITARY CAREER

9th April 1789: became an ensign in 38th Foot, serving in Ireland where he met Arthur Wellesley, later Duke of Wellington.
1791-95: promoted in several regiments, serving in Flanders, was wounded at Famers, later fought at Dunkirk, Valenciennes, Nieuwpoort and Tournai and was in the retreat to Bremen.
August 1795: served with the 53rd Foot in Barbados. Took part in the capture of St Lucia and Trinidad, the suppression of civil disorder on St Vincent and the failed invasion of Puerto Rico, returning home on sick leave in 1798. He was fortunate – many regiments lost over 90% of their strength to yellow fever.
1800: appointed Lieutenant Colonel of the 69th Foot and sailed for Jamaica. Left in 1803 on sick leave; did not go with his regiment to India in 1805 because of ill health.
1810: promoted Colonel, serving with the York Rangers. After 18 months as Assistant Adjutant General in the Peninsula, he took command of the 1st Brigade of Picton's 3rd Division with the rank of Brigadier-General, leading the brigade at the battles of Vittoria, the Pyrenees, Nivelle, Nive, Orthez and Toulouse where he was once again wounded.
1813: advanced to Major-General and was decorated for his Peninsular service.
1814: appointed KCB, he reached Canada with reinforcements, commanding a brigade during General George Prevost's abortive attack on the American stronghold of Plattsburg, thus missing Waterloo, although he did command a division in the army of occupation in France until 1818.
[1821-25 Governor of New South Wales and Van Diemen's Land].
27th May 1825: promoted Lieutenant General.
16th December 1826: appointed Colonel of the 34th Foot, which he held until his death in 1860
23rd November 1841: promoted General.

ASTRONOMY AND GEOPHYSICS

1798: Brisbane was nearly shipwrecked on his way back from Jamaica , which led to his developing navigation at sea through the stars.
1808: he built Brisbane Observatory near Brisbane House in Largs. It had three clocks and Troughton's 2 foot mural circle (which was the first of its kind and a model for the 6 foot circle installed at Greenwich Observatory).
During the Peninsular War he took regular observations with a pocket sextant, helping to navigate the fleet and prompting Wellington to remark that 'he kept the time of the army'.
1810: became a member of the Royal Society of London (vice-President 1827).
1818: during the occupation of France Wellington asked him to compute a table determining time from the altitudes of heavenly bodies and also to draw up a comparison of English weights and measures with French ones.
1821: Brisbane took his instruments with him to NSW observing Encke's comet and the transit of Mercury. A catalogue of 7,385 stars mostly in the southern hemisphere was prepared at his observatory at Parramatta in Australia. (His Parramatta observatory was demolished in 1855 and an obelisk erected in 1880).
1826: built Makerstoun Observatory with an adjacent magnetic laboratory in 1841 (for years the only one in Scotland) as part of Gauss's Geomagnetic Union. The shell of his observatory at Largs remains, while Makerstoun's astronomical observatory building was restored in 1986/7.
1828: received the gold medal of the Astronomical Society from Sir John Herschel.
1832: succeeded Sir Walter Scott as President of the Royal Society of Edinburgh, endowing a Royal Society 'Brisbane Biennial' medal. Honorary degrees were awarded by Oxford (1832) Cambridge (1833), Edinburgh (1834).
1834: presided over the meeting of the British Association for the Advancement of Science in Edinburgh.
1848: Royal Society of Edinburgh's Keith Medal for his work at Makerstoun
1860: died at Brisbane House in the room where he was born.

Born in Kelso on 5th January 1816, James Brunlees attended the Parish School before transferring to Mr Scott's private school. There he excelled in arithmetic and basic measuring. He left school at the age of 12 to follow his father's profession as a gardener and steward with a view to becoming a landscape gardener at Broomlands. However he had a natural taste for engineering work.

Broomlands at that time was occupied by Mr Innes, agent to the Duke of Roxburghe. Through Innes, Brunlees met the civil engineer Alexander J. Adie, who was carrying out work on the Roxburghe Estates. Brunlees picked up a considerable knowledge of surveying, and was eventually employed to make a survey of the estates. During this time he saved money to pay for classes at Edinburgh University, where he studied for several sessions. Mr Adie continued to employ James, and in 1838 engaged him in the construction of the Bolton and Preston Railway. It was in Bolton he met Elizabeth Kirkman who became his wife.

Brunlees moved on to construct a section of the *Caledonian Railway* from Beattock to Carstairs. He then moved to the Stalybridge branch of the *Lancashire and Yorkshire Railway* under Sir John Hawkshaw. In 1850 Brunlees set up his own practice, becoming engineer to the *Londonderry and Coleraine Railway* in Ireland. This involved the construction of embankments under difficult conditions across Rosse's Bay in the River Foyle. Brunlees's success here helped him obtain the appointment as engineer to the *Ulverston and Lancaster Railway*.

His reputation had gained universal acclaim and Baron de Maua, principal concessionaire in Brazil, engaged him in the survey and construction of the *San Paulo Railway* in 1857. On completion of this work the Emperor of Brazil presented James Brunlees with the Order of the Rose.

Despite his international fame James Brunlees never forgot his native soil. He frequently returned to Kelso for holidays,

Southend Pier, picture courtesy Southend-on-Sea Borough Council.

to fish and shoot. A skilful and successful angler, he had an outstanding record for catching salmon at Sprouston and Hempseedford. In 1854 the police commissioners asked him to design new sewerage and water systems for the town of Kelso and this he did for the cost of the outlay on plans and specifications, declining payment for much of the work. The first drains were laid from Horsemarket along Shedden Park Road to the Tweed. For many years, James Brunlees was President of Kelso's Mechanics Institute and took a keen interest in it, giving frequent donations of books and, on occasion, sums of money for essay prizes.

The *Channel Tunnel Railway Company* was incorporated in 1872 and Brunlees once again worked with Sir John Hawkshaw, planning a railway link between England and France. The Company folded in 1886, a full hundred years before the tunnel became a reality. However a deviation of no more than a few inches was the result when Brunlees along with Douglas Fox, the resident engineer started work at Liverpool and Birkenhead and met almost exactly in the middle to form *The Mersey Tunnel*.

Throughout his career, the design of iron structures for tidal waters was a continuing theme. Brunlees was responsible for impressive examples of seaside piers, at Llandudno, New Brighton, Southport, and Southend, the longest pleasure pier in the world at 1.33 miles. As engineer to the Solway Junction Railway he designed an iron viaduct across the firth 1¼ miles long.

Brunlees became a Council member of the Institute of Civil Engineers in 1865 and President in 1882-3. Queen Victoria awarded him a knighthood in 1886. Brunlees died at his home, Argyle Lodge, Wimbledon on 2nd June 1892.

Peter Crawford

1818-1889

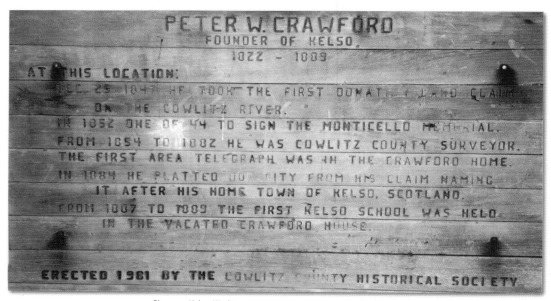

PETER W. CRAWFORD
FOUNDER OF KELSO.
1822 - 1889

AT THIS LOCATION:
DEC 25 1847 HE TOOK THE FIRST DONATION LAND CLAIM
ON THE COWLITZ RIVER.
IN 1852 ONE OF 44 TO SIGN THE MONTICELLO MEMORIAL.
FROM 1854 TO 1882 HE WAS COWLITZ COUNTY SURVEYOR.
THE FIRST AREA TELEGRAPH WAS IN THE CRAWFORD HOME.
IN 1884 HE PLATTED OUR CITY FROM HIS CLAIM NAMING
IT AFTER HIS HOME TOWN OF KELSO. SCOTLAND.
FROM 1887 TO 1889 THE FIRST KELSO SCHOOL WAS HELD
IN THE VACATED CRAWFORD HOUSE.

ERECTED 1981 BY THE COWLITZ COUNTY HISTORICAL SOCIETY

Plaque at Kelso, Washington picture courtesy Margaret Riddell MBE.

Kelso Washington Police badge, notice the motto!

The State seat of government at Oregon City was a long way from Cowlitz and largely ignored the needs of their northern settlers. They moved that the territory be divided at the Columbia River and in 1853 the territory of Washington, named after George, was formed. Peter married and the family moved to Vancouver to seek medical treatment for their elder daughter whose health was poor. Their farm at Cowlitz was turned into a platted city of 500 lots and named KELSO. In 1887 the Crawford's former house was converted into a school. The brothers donated lots to encourage businesses to locate to Kelso, as well as for an academy and a Presbyterian Church.

Washington Territory decided to join the Union as a State and Crawford re-surveyed the town of Kelso to enable it to be an incorporated city, dying the following year in 1889. One of the new council's first acts was to name a street in his honour.

Peter Crawford was born in Sprouston near Kelso in 1818 and educated in Kelso before training as a surveyor in Edinburgh. In 1843 he joined his elder brother, Alexander, in Indiana. He then accompanied George Cline and family on a wagon train bound for Oregon, arriving there in 1847. The Hudson's Bay Company had responded to a recent treaty between Britain and the United States by withdrawing from the farmlands around the Cowlitz River. The Canadians had hoped to make the Columbia River their boundary and were suspected of encouraging Indian attacks so as to deter American settlers on the north bank of the river.

Crawford located a land claim on the northern bank beside the Cowlitz (at that time part of the state of Oregon) and then moved on to make the first survey for the town of Vancouver on the Columbia River. In 1849 Crawford had some success prospecting for gold in California, but returned to Cowlitz where his brother Alexander and a friend Victor Wallace had proved adjacent claims. During the 1850s as well as being the first surveyor of Cowlitz (an area which was becoming thickly populated) he platted the towns of Vancouver, Astoria, Milwaukie, Ranier, St. Helens, Columbia City and Sauvies Island. He was to return to Cowlitz where he built a house.

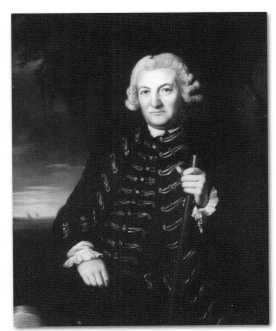

James Dickson, picture courtesy of Ednam House Hotel

James Dickson was born in Stichell, the son of a tenant farmer. Aged about fourteen, young James was apprenticed to a saddler in Kelso. However, he seems to have been a high spirited and mischievous young man for he vandalised the Town Well in the Square, (according to one version by polluting it with a dead cat), then fled the town to escape from punishment.

The details of his subsequent career are somewhat obscure but by 1739 he was living in London where he carved out a very successful career as a merchant. It is likely that among his activities he was a prize agent dealing with the sale of ships captured during the wars with France and Spain. (At that time enemy ships and their contents were sold and the spoils shared by the men who had captured them.) He probably also did very well from the capture of Havannah in Cuba in 1762, as he would later name his house after this event.

In the 1760's James Dickson returned to his native town, now an extremely wealthy man. He immediately began to acquire land in the district including an area beside the River Tweed, between Oven Wynd and the Old Bridge. Here he built himself a handsome town house - Havannah House - employing as his architect one James Nisbet, also a native of Kelso but with a practice in London. He also bought a number of properties in the Square where he had the Cross Keys Hotel erected. Further afield he bought the barony of Broughton near Peebles, and he became Member of Parliament for a Scottish Burghs seat.

In 1765 James Dickson bought the barony of Ednam from the last of the Edmonstone lairds. Thereafter he styled himself Dickson of Ednam and his house in Kelso was renamed Ednam House. As laird he was an enthusiastic improver, draining and enclosing land, building a water powered mill for making woollen cloth, and encouraging the setting up of a brewery business. The village of Ednam was rebuilt, the houses being roofed with pantiles or slates, and its main street is still today as Dickson planned it. His most ambitious project - for a canal from Kelso to Berwick to allow for the easier export of local produce - was never achieved. He was unable to raise the enthusiasm, or the money, from other local landowners and the plan came to nothing. He died in 1771, aged just 59.

Ednam House

George Henry Scott Douglas

1825-1885

Sir George Henry Scott Douglas was born in Edinburgh on 19 June 1825. He was the eldest of four children and the only son of Sir John James Scott Douglas of Springwood Park, Kelso and Hannah Charlotte Scott of Belford. His father died when he was just 11 and he succeeded to his father's estates and titles at that time. He was a pupil at Harrow school. His military career began with him briefly entering the navy and then joining the 34th Regiment of Foot (The Border Regiment).

Sir George Henry Scott Douglas picture courtesy of the Heritage Hub.

Sir George chronicled his early military career in his diaries. In 1845 aged 19 he was stationed at Athlone Ireland. By October that year he had set sail for Corfu. It was when based there at he purchased his first yacht the Cutter *Vampire*. He obtained leave and sailed around the Mediterranean. During this time he chronicled his travels in a vivid account. His stay in the army was a brief period (he resigned his commission in 1851) of his career but during that time he reached the rank of Captain.

While in Gibraltar he met his future wife Mariquita the eldest daughter of Don Francisco Serrano Sanchez De Pina of Gibraltar. They had six children although one son died in infancy. The eldest son James who was expected to become the fifth Baronet was killed on 3 July 1879 whilst

Douglas Family History

The Douglas family owned the estate of Springwood Park in Kelso for six generations.

The family can trace its origins back to James, first Earl of Douglas and Mar, who died in 1384, from whom descended the Douglases of Cavers. A later descendant, William Douglas acquired the lands of Friarshaw in the parishes of Bowden and Lilliesleaf and the family now titled itself 'of Friarshaw'.

The first Baronet James Douglas, (1704-1787) had a distinguished career in the Royal Navy, after which, he retired as an Admiral. He was created a baronet in 1786 and then a Knight of the Order of the Bath. In 1750, he bought the estate of Bridge End, and renamed it Springwood Park. Sir James went on to serve as the MP for Orkney and Shetland (1754-61 and

✔ Categories

> Casts anchor (1)
> Destruction of wildlife (3)
> Drunk (1)
> Feeling seedy (1)
> Introduction (1)
> Near misses (1)
> Sets sail (3)
> Uncategorized (7)

View his travels at www.voyageofthevampire.org.uk

serving with the army in Zululand and it was the second son George Brisbane Douglas who succeeded to the baronetcy.

After he left the army and settled down to life in Kelso he became actively involved in local life. He served as the Conservative MP for Roxburghshire between 1874-1880, he also was a magistrate and briefly served on the first school board for Kelso. He was also involved in Tweedside Physical and Antiquarian Society and contributed to their museum and was president of the Kelso curling club.

He kept a connection to his former life in the army by serving in the Kelso volunteer movement. He was the first captain of the Kelso company and took a leading part in organising the Roxburgh and Selkirk battalion. Following the death of Lord Polwarth in 1867 he was appointed Lieutenant-Colonel. He was also President of the Border Rifle Association.

Sir George passed away on 26 June 1885 shortly after his 60th birthday.

Sir William Fairbairn – picture SCRAN

Born 3rd March 1789, in a house at the corner of Roxburgh Street and Chalkheugh Terrace, Kelso commemorated by a plaque.

William Fairbairn attended a private school run by Mr Ker, before attending the English school under Mr. White. His grandfather was a gardener to the Baillies of Mellerstain. His father Andrew Fairbairn, a farmer served in the Navy during the American War of Independence. Margaret Fairbairn,

his mother was the daughter of a Jedburgh tradesman and she clothed the family by her efforts at the spinning wheel, making and dyeing cloth, blankets and shirting.

William began at an early age to demonstrate his construction skills by building boats and little mills. From an uncle living in Galashiels, William learned book-keeping and land surveying. He obtained work on the construction of Kelso Bridge. However he suffered an injury when a huge stone rolled onto his leg.

The family moved to North Shields, where his father obtained employment as a land steward. William became apprenticed to a millwright at Newcastle. However he read avidly and continued his mathematical and other studies, by educating himself from libraries. Because of this technical ingenuity he was appointed to look after engines at the Percy Main colliery, where he became acquainted with George Stephenson.

Moving to London in 1811 he secured an introduction to the Society of Arts and to Alexander Tilloch who was the founder of the Philosophical Magazine. Tilloch employed him in the construction of a steam engine to be used for digging. In 1817 he set up in partnership with James Lillie to provide machinery for cotton mills. They also made water wheels for the Catrine Cotton Works in Ayrshire and built a light iron steamship to work on the Forth and Clyde Canal. In 1824, Fairbairn went to Zurich to erect 2 watermills, surmounting the problem of irregular water supply by constructing wheels which worked regularly whatever the river height.

When the recession hit the cotton industry Fairbairn moved in to the locomotive boiler manufacture, where he greatly improved steam boilers and often was called as an expert witness if deaths had occurred due to a boiler explosion. He invented the riveting machine which enabled factories to speed up their operations. His diversification after the cotton recession also led him to shipbuilding.

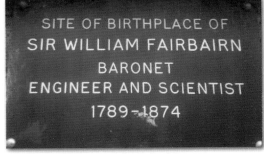

Plaque on wall in Roxburgh Street

He constructed over 80 vessels for the Peninsular and Oriental Company and others for the British Government introducing iron shipbuilding to the River Thames. This experience led him to conceive the idea of a rectangular tube or box girder to bridge the large gap between Anglesey and North Wales.

Fairbairn was elected President of the Institution of Mechanical engineers in 1854. He often spoke at the British Association and served as a juror in the London exhibitions of 1851 and 1852, receiving the Gold Medal of the Royal Society of London for the Improvement of Natural Knowledge (known as Royal Society) in 1860. He also served as a juror at the Paris exhibition in 1855. He was made a member of the Légion d'honneur in 1855 and also became a foreign member of the Institut de France.

Fairbairn declined a knighthood in 1861; however he accepted a baronetcy in 1869. When he died in 1874, 50,000 people attended his funeral. He is buried at Prestwick, Northumberland.

John Forrest

1797-1869

John Forrest was born in Jedburgh, the youngest of three sons of blacksmith William Forrest and Ann Wood. In 1809, John's eldest brother, George, helped their father to set up a gunsmith's business in Jedburgh and George's sons became gunsmiths in their turn.

John spent several years in the merchant navy. It was almost certainly during his years at sea that he began to think about and experiment with the making of fishing rods. In the early days, before previously unknown woods began to be imported from the colonies, fishing rods were home-made using local woods such as hazel, crab and juniper. John's service overseas introduced him to exotic woods such as greenheart, lancewood and bamboo. Greenheart, grown in South America, was to become the most popular wood for rod making because it is so dense and heavy and one of the strongest woods known.

One great advantage was that it could be cut down to a very fine, but still strong tip. It also resists decay and was often used for repairing canal gates and piers.

In 1837, John and his brother George set up their fishing tackle business in Kelso Square, trading as Forrest & Sons. While George brought his gunmaking expertise to the tackle making side of the business, John's true skills lay in the making of the rods. To begin with, every fishing rod that John sold was entirely his own making – from the sawing of the wood to its final completion. John's reputation for fine craftsmanship spread through the British Empire and the firm became so successful that over 100 outworkers were employed. John was also a fine violin maker.

John's youngest son, George, took over the business (two of his brothers and all three sisters had died young). He too, was a master rod maker and gunsmith. In 1886 George Forrest entered a competition for Fly Fishing and Greenheart Fishing Rods at the Colonial and Indian Exhibition in London in 1886 The firm was awarded two Gold and three Silver medals.

Forrest of Kelso still trades today from 1 Bridge Street Kelso.

Forrest and Sons, Kelso

William Glass of Tristan da Cunha

Governor Glass

William Glass or Glasgow was born in Kelso on 11th May 1786, to David and Janet Glasgow who lived in the Townhead area of the town at the top of Roxburgh Street. In March 1804 he enlisted in the British Army at Berwick-on-Tweed as a gun driver for the Royal Artillery. He gave his name as William Glass not Glasgow, claimed to be 16 years old not 18, and described himself as an ordinary labourer, although later in life he would claim to have been a servant at Floors Castle. Why did he leave home under an assumed name? Was there some dark secret in his past? Who knows?

He did quite well in the army rising to the rank of corporal of artillery. In 1816 he was part of a garrison sent by the British

Government from Capetown in South Africa, to take control of the tiny island of Tristan da Cunha in the South Atlantic. Napoleon Bonaparte had been sent into exile on St Helena after his final defeat at Waterloo, but it was feared there might be an attempt by his supporters to rescue him, and Tristan might be used as a base from which to mount the attack. However, the danger died down and in 1817 the garrison was withdrawn.

The remote island lost in the South Atlantic must have appealed to William Glass, for he and another man requested permission to settle on the island, and this was granted by Lord Somerset, governor of Cape Colony. In November 1817 Glass brought over his South African wife, Maria Magdalena Leenders (of mixed Dutch/Hottentot race) and their two children to Tristan. They also had a bull, a cow and several sheep. They were joined by several other men, but Glass was the only one who was married, until in 1827 five women from St Helena were persuaded to come to the island to make life more agreeable for the bachelors. The population continued to grow with the addition of a Dutchman, Peter Groen or Green, and a couple of Americans Thomas Rogers and Andrew Hagan from whaling ships. Glass and his wife had sixteen children - eight sons and eight daughters. By 1852 there were 85 people living in the settlement.

Glass ran the settlement in a patriarchal fashion until his death in 1853. His rules were based on equality with all land communally owned and everyone having an equal share of the livestock and supplies. The rules he drew up are still the basis for the crofting life-style of the present inhabitants.

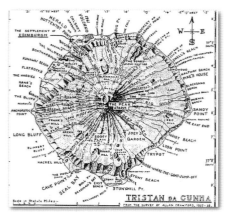

Map of Tristan da Cunha

He was also a devout Christian, who held two Church of England services every Sunday. His firm authority ensured that intoxication and quarrelling were not allowed, not only among the islanders but also among the crews of passing whaling ships. He seems to have been a man of good education who taught the island's children himself.

Every Christmas there was a family gathering for dinner: it is recorded that on the last such occasion in 1852 he was surrounded by 33 members of his family including 19 grandchildren. His descendants still live on the island today.

images courtesy of www.britishempire.co.uk

The Administrator's House

In Malaya he developed a reputation as one of the best boxers in the British Armed Forces, winning the title of Far East Armed Forces light heavy-weight champion.

When he came back to Kelso he returned to work as a joiner. Later he became repairman on the British railways line squads.

He joined Kelso RFC as a prop, captaining the side and playing for the South of Scotland along with his brother Arthur. He was married in 1955 to Loretta and in that year he won his first cap for Scotland against France. His greatest moment came in a 1958 match against France at Murrayfield, when after catching an astute throw from Arthur Smith, Hastie drove over the line. His try was decisive in the teams eventual 11-9 victory.

1964 saw the railway closures under Beeching. He decided to emigrate to New Zealand with his wife and three children. He worked on the railways first of all on South Island them for most of his career in Lower Hutt, near Wellington. There he shunted wagons around the busy docks of Wellington.

Whilst in Kelso he had been a talented darts player and this he continued in his new life, gaining caps for New Zealand.

Ian Robert Hastie was born in Kelso on September 7th 1929. He was the son of a popular local cabinet maker. He attended the Abbey School – now Abbey Row Centre and then during the war years Kelso High School.

After leaving school, he became an apprentice joiner, until compulsory national service took him to the conflict in Malaya. He served as an infantryman with the 1st Battalion Cameronians. There he saw combat in the jungle against communist guerrillas. The endless nights spent in insect infested jungles left him with sores, which were to affect him for the rest of his life.

Photograph courtesy of Friends of Kelso Museum.

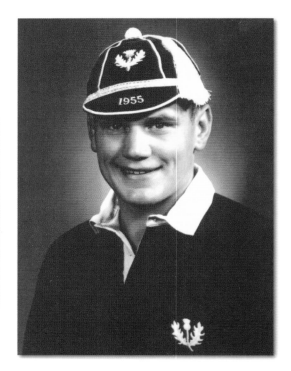

View from site of Jerdan's House.

a pupil of Dr. Rutherford's at Maxwellheugh, and this led to his choice of literature as a profession. On leaving school, he entered the office of James Hume, W.S., but soon went to try his fortune in London and in 1801 obtained a clerkship in the counting-house of Turner, West Indian merchants. This was cut short when, a year later, he developed brain fever and returned to Scotland, to a position with Cornelius Scott, W.S., Edinburgh. Not finding this congenial, he headed south once more.

In the spring of 1806, Jerdan settled in London and began his journalistic career by joining staff of the "Aurora", a morning paper. He became editor, but when the "Aurora" failed he transferred to the "Pilot", an evening paper. He next joined the staff of the "Morning Post"

Lang Linkie was a 16th Century house standing in Roxburgh Street, Kelso, overlooking the junction of Tweed and Teviot – a site now occupied by the supermarket. Here, on 16th April 1782, William Jerdan was born. He attended the Parish School and then moved on to the Grammar School where he was taught Greek and Latin. His teacher was the eminent Dr. John Dymock, whose educational and classical works were later reviewed by Jerdan in the Literary Gazette. As a child William developed smallpox and, to aid his recovery, he was given a cold bath in the Tweed which left him in a delicate state of health for years. A bright scholar, William was selected as companion/boarder for

and reported the proceedings of Parliament. On this duty on the afternoon of 12th May, 1812, he was in the lobby of the House of Commons when the Prime Minister, Spencer Perceval, passed with a smile of recognition. Perceval had been Chancellor of the Exchequer under Portland and retained this post in his own administration. A bankrupt called Bellingham, who had a grudge against the government, fired a pistol and Perceval fell dead between the pillars. In Jerdan's own words: "It is very remarkable to state, that, though I was all but touching him and if the ball had passed through his body it must have lodged in mine I did not hear the report of the pistol. I saw a small curling

wreath of smoke rise above his head as if the breath of a cigar; I saw him reel back against the ledge on the inside of the door; I heard him exclaim 'Oh God' and nothing more." Jerdan was first to apprehend the assassin.

Later in 1812, Jerdan purchased the copyright and business premises – 267 The Strand – of the "Satirist, a monthly Meteor", but it was not a commercial success and ceased in 1814. Meanwhile, he had become the editor of the "Sun", a high Tory daily newspaper, and gave literary work some prominence in its columns, unusual in a daily paper of that time. His connection with the "Sun" gave him acquaintance with some of the chief Tory statesmen and in 1819 George Canning, later to become Prime Minister, became godfather to one of his sons.

The "Sun" was unprofitable and Jerdan retired from the editor-ship and sold his interest in the concern in 1817. Two months later, Jerdan was installed as editor of a news weekly review, "The Literary Gazette", and was identified with this enterprise for 33 years. At first he supplemented his income by contributions to the provincial press and, from London, he edited the "Sheffield Mercury", among others. In 1820 Longmans became part-proprietors and publishers of the Gazette, and for the next 10 years it, and Jerdan, held a supreme position in the literary world, his connection lasting until 1850. He moved into a larger house called "The Grove" at Old Brompton. In 1821, Jerdan assisted in founding the Royal Society of Literature and took a prominent part in administering the literary fund. He was also presented with a testimonial, subscribed to by leading figures of the day, as "a public acknowledgement of his services to literature, science, the fine and useful arts". William Jerdan died at Bushey Heath on 11th July, 1869.

Thora Ker

Thora Ker was born in Kelso, her father being William Ker, Watchmaker and Jeweller. Thora attended the Infants School in Inch Road and then Kelso High School. Her highest achievements were in Art and Music. She was greatly influenced by her art teachers and music teachers-all very fine artists. Her ambition was to be an actress, appearing in plays at school from as early as primary school. However, in those days one was encouraged to be a teacher or a nurse so Drama School was not an option. Her first stage appearance, for Kelso Operatic society at Kelso Tait Hall, was at the age of five as one of the little children in the King and I.

Influenced greatly by her mother and her Auntie Ruth who were heavily involved with Kelso Amateur Operatic and Dramatic Societies, Thora continued to perform in plays at high school, sing locally in churches and also in a pop group at school. Her musical talents shone through as she played the organ in the country churches for St. John's Parish and performed in three operas at school with Fergus Malcolm and Grace Payne (music teachers). The third being in her final year at school when she sang the role of the mother in Menotti's Amahl and the Night Visitors.

Thora then studied at the Royal Scottish Academy of Music and Drama and St. Andrew's College, Glasgow, winning several major prizes and scholarships. She made her operatic debut with Scottish Opera, performing the role of Selina in Weber's OBERON, receiving the John Scott Award and being selected for the National Opera Studio,

London. Since then, Thora has become recognised as a consumate actress and highly musical singer performing principal mezzo roles with most of the major British Opera Companies and working with Britain's leading producers and conductors.

Her operatic roles include Pitti-Sing The Mikado (English National Opera), Blanche The Gambler (ENO), Minerva and Love Return of Ulysses (ENO) and Kate Pinkerton Madame Butterfly (ENO). Siebel Faust (Opera North), Cherubino Marriage of Figaro (Scottish Opera), Schoolboy/Groom Lulu (SO), Dorabella Cosi Fan Tutte (Garsington Manor and Orleans Festival, France), Second Lady The Magic Flute (Dublin Grand Opera), Serafina Il Campanello (Les Azuriales Opera, France), Elisetta Il Matrimonio Segreto (Les Azuriales Opera), Phoebe Yeoman of the Guard, Tessa The Gondoliers, Iolanthe, Pitti-Sing The Mikado and Lady Angela Patience, for the Carl Rosa Opera. Other performances include the lead mezzo roles in the world premiere of Kenneth Leighton's Columba, Theatre Royal, Glasgow, The sixty minute Cinderella (The Royal Opera), Carmen, Don Giovanni, The Beggars Opera, Die Fledermaus, La Traviata, Riders to the sea, The rape of Lucretia, Mrs MacMotherly and Dame Cherry Maybud Ages Ago at the Linbury Studio, Covent Garden, and for Opera à la Carte, Welsh National Opera and the Royal Opera Education Programmes.

Thora is a founder member of the new D'Oyly Carte Opera and sang Phoebe, Yeoman of the Guard, the title-role Iolanthe, and Pitti-Sing, which she has recorded with TER Records, Sony Classical's The Best of Gilbert and Sullivan, and performed in Los Angeles.

Her versatility and wide ranging repertoire across the fields of opera, operetta, oratorio, lieder, Scots song, ballad and the musicals has been highlighted in her guest appearances, on peak-time entertainment programmes, with BBC Television, Scottish Television. She performed in a special New Year's Eve edition of 'Highway' with the late Sir Harry Secombe for Border and other ITV Networks, in Hogmanay and Christmas Specials for Border and Central ITV, on BBC Radio Scotland, Radio Forth and BBC Radio 2's 'Friday Night is Music Night'. She has recorded a selection of songs on CD: 'Festival of Music 1999' and '100th Anniversary of the RAF, 2008' with the world famous Central Band of the RAF, and has her own solo album of popular favourites entitled 'Thora'.

Thora's international solo career has taken her on two extensive tours of Canada and America, to Italy and the Low Countries. In concert and oratorio she has made solo guest appearances in auditoriums and theatres such as the famous Hollywood Bowl, the Willshire Ebell Theatre, Los Angeles; Hamilton Place, Ontario; the Jubilee Auditoriums in Calgary and Edmonton; the Orpheum Theatre, Vancouver; the Palais des Beaux-Arts, Brussels; the Royal Albert Hall, the Royal Festival Hall, the Barbican and in most of the major theatres and concert halls in the UK. She has given a series of solo recitals at the Royal Opera House, the Schubert Society, and for the Friends of the Royal Opera and Scottish Opera.

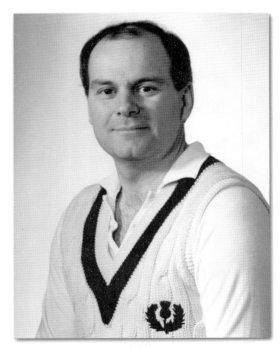

Jack Ker

John Edward Patrick Ker (Jack) one of Scotland's foremost cricket stars, was born in Kelso on 17th October 1952. His brother, Andrew Burgher Michael Ker, born on 16th October 1954, played cricket and rugby for Scotland. Their father Andrew had played cricket, badminton and tennis to good levels and Uncle Will was a good cricketer and international umpire. Younger sister Patsy was to become a South hockey player. As boys, Jack and Michael quickly developed a great rivalry turning their cul-de-sac at Abbey Court into a series of sporting venues.

Jack's teen years were spent mainly on the football field with Kelso United and Duns where he caught the interest of Hibernian and Aston Villa. However, after finishing a football match, Jack went with friends to Hawick to watch his brother help Kelso to win the Hawick Sevens. The next week he was at Poynder Park and was to play centre (occasionally stand-off and full-back) in the Kelso Ist XV for the next three years. Jack a gifted all-rounder, having a golf handicap of four and excelling at badminton, was picked to play cricket for Scotland. Unfortunately, the match clashed with his final PE exams at Jordanhill College and he had to turn down the chance. It was five years before he was selected by Scotland again, during which he helped Kelso and Heriot's to league titles. In his first match for Scotland, he bowled David Gower with his very first ball and also scored a run with his first ball. He also bowled the legendary Indian trio of Sunil Gavaskar (again first ball), Mohammad Azharuddin and Dilip Vengsarkar playing for Scotland in two one-day internationals at Dumfries and scored 50 against New Zealand in Dundee. In his 10 years playing for Scotland, he won 57 caps retiring in 1987.

Andrew played rugby for Kelso High School and Kelso Ist XV before being selected for South of Scotland, Scotland 'B' and the full Scotland side. He followed his brother to Jordanhill College. He had won the first of 22 Scotland cricket caps against Australia in 1981 and it was against Australia that he first sat on the rugby bench for Scotland in 1984. He was in competition with John Rutherford for the Scotland no. 10 jersey, which he finally achieved at the age of 33. Between 1973 and 1990 Andrew was one of Scotland's brightest stars on the rugby sevens circuit, winning 43 Border Sevens tournaments, finishing runner-up a further 13 and representing Scotland around the world.

Andrew Ker

Henry Francis Lyte

1793-1847

Henry Francis Lyte
Picture courtesy www.portoraroyal.co.uk

Henry Francis Lyte was born in 'The Cottage' in Ednam on 1st June 1793, the second son of Captain Thomas Lyte of the Royal Marines and his wife Anna Maria Oliver. The family lived for a number of years in Ednam, but Captain Lyte was drafted to Ireland after the rebellion in 1798 and the rest of the family followed soon after. Here Henry and his older brother Thomas were entered as pupils at Portora Royal School in Enniskillen. However, soon after this the family broke up. Captain Lyte abandoned his family and went to Jersey. His wife and her youngest child George moved to London where they both soon died. What became of older brother Thomas is uncertain. What is clear is that at the age of nine, Henry found himself alone without a family to support him.

Fortunately the headmaster of Portora, Dr Robert Burrows, took pity on the young orphan. He recognised that Henry was a very able boy and took charge of him effectively adopting him, taking him into his family and paying for his continuing education at Portora.

Lyte worked hard and in 1809 he won a scholarship to Trinity College, Dublin where he studied Divinity. He was a brilliant scholar, and was also emerging as a talented poet winning the Chancellor's prize for English verse three years in a row. He graduated in 1814. The following year he was ordained as a clergyman in the Episcopalian Church. He served first as Curate at Taghmon in Ireland but his health was fragile - he suffered for much of his life from lung trouble - and after a holiday in France and Italy for his health, he took up a post at Marazion in the gentler climate of Cornwall. It was here that he met his wife Anne Maxwell, daughter of a fellow churchman and they married in 1818.

In 1823 he became the curate of Brixham where he was a much loved minister for many years until his final illness. He worked hard, writing many hymns, prayers for the use of sailors, metrical versions of the Psalms, and books of mainly religious poetry. Some of his most famous works were *Praise, my soul, the King of Heaven*, based on Psalm 103, *God of Mercy, God of Grace*, based on Psalm 67 and of course the famous hymn *Abide with me!* which he wrote during his last illness.

Plaque at Ednam

Henry Lyte's health had been poor for many years and he developed what in those days was called consumption – we would call it tuberculosis. Following a serious illness in 1839 he was ordered by his doctor to rest. He spent several winters abroad for the sake of his health but in 1847, on 20th November, he died at Nice in the south of France. Just before his departure from Britain he had started work on his greatest hymn *Abide with me!*. The final version was sent home from Avignon, shortly before his death. Since 1927 it has been sung every year at the F.A. cup final at Wembley Stadium.

Although he never returned to Scotland, Lyte never forgot his early childhood in Ednam. A plaque in Ednam churchyard commemorates his life.

Abide With Me

Abide with me;
Fast falls the eventide.
The darkness deepens,
Lord with me abide.
When other helpers fail
And comforts flee,
Help of the helpless,
Oh, abide with me.

Ednam

Born 16th June 1950, at the long demolished prefabs at Inchmyre, Kelso, Alistair Murray Moffat has become synonymous with Border literature.

The son of Jack and Ellen Moffat, Kelso the family moved from the prefabs to 42 Inchmead Drive. Alistair and his two sisters attended Inch Road Infants School known to him as *The Prison*.

Starting as a ball boy whilst still at Primary School he progressed to playing against the under 16s Welsh schools team, inspired by his father's note – *Remember where you come from* - he *"tackled every Welsh man who came near me"*, unfortunately they lost 6:3. He played for Kelso First XV being picked out by Norman Mair as *a promising player along with Wattie Blake, the best in the Kelso pack.*

Working after school earning 7/6d a week helping Tommy Pontin deliver the Store milk he bought a KB Dansette record player with his hard earned cash. Later he turned his hand to delivering newspapers in North Kelso.

After leaving Kelso High School, Alistair attended St Andrews University, where he gained an MA Hons, furthering his studies at Edinburgh University (Cert.Ed.) and London University (MPhil).

In 1976 he began a five-year period in charge of the Edinburgh Festival Fringe. This experience resulted in the publication of his first book, *The Edinburgh Fringe*, in 1978. He then moved to Scottish Television and rose through the ranks to become Director of Programmes and Chief Executive of Network Production.

Returning to the Borders to live he became the Director of the Borders Book Festival which takes place in Melrose each summer and is growing in popularity every year.

The author of thirteen titles, including *Kelsae: A History of Kelso from Earliest Times* which was originally published in 1985 and updated and reprinted in 2006.

His book, *The Borders*, the definitive history of the Borders, was published in paperback in May 2007. The *Reivers* published by Birlinn in June 2007, accompanied a six-part television series, which was commissioned and broadcast by Border Television and presented by Alistair and a fellow descendant of the Reivers, Fiona Armstrong.

Alistair's book *The Wall*: was published in conjunction with a major 6-part ITV series presented by Alistair and Dame Tanni-Grey Thompson.

In addition to his books he has also produced numerous DVDs featuring his beloved Border land including *"Walking the line"*, which explores the Border and involved walking the 108 miles from the Solway to Berwick.

Titles:

The Edinburgh Fringe	1978
Kelsae: a history of Kelso from earliest times	1985 reprinted 2006
Remembering Charles Rennie Mackintosh	1989
Arthur and the Lost Kingdoms	1999
The Sea Kingdoms	2001
The Borders	2002
Heartland	2004
Homing	2003
Before Scotland	2005
Tyneside	2006
East Lothian	2006
The Reivers	2007
Fife; A History	2007
The Wall	2008
Edinburgh: A Short History	2008

William Henry Ogilvie

1869-1963

William Henry Ogilvie was born at Holefield, Kelso on 21st August 1869. At that time his father was tenant of the farm which was owned by the Duke of Buccleuch. His grandfather was chamberlain to the Duke and lived at Branxholme near Hawick. His mother's parents had been killed in a massacre at Cawnpore in India when she was a child.

William Henry Ogilvie

As a small child Will, along with his brothers and sisters, was taught by a governess at home. He was the eldest son and second child in a family of eight. For a short time he was sent to Yorkshire to be tutored by a clergyman. After a term at Kelso High School as a day boarder, he attended Fettes College where he studied Greek and Latin, winning the school prize for Latin verse. However, he also excelled on the sports field, playing rugby for the College 1st XV.

At the age of nineteen he was sent to Australia to help friends of the family, the Scotts of Belalie, who had a large sheep station. It was fashionable at that time for aspiring young farmers to emigrate to the young colony where the wool trade was booming. It appears that he had a deep love of horses, wild buckjumpers as the drovers called them. He stayed in Australia for twelve years working at Belalie and Maroupe Station in South Australia. Whilst learning about droving he also learned a lot about observation and writing which was the foundation for his poetry.

In Australia, he began to write romantic and lyrical poetry known for its balladic style. He was renowned in Australia and was considered comparable with the native writers of that time Banjo Patterson, Henry Lawson and Adam Lindsay Gordon.

He returned to Scotland in 1901 and lived in Edinburgh for a short time, during this period he was offered a post in America. This was a dual role, as the chair of Agricultural Journalism at the State College of Iowa and Editor of the *Experimental Station*. However he soon discovered that academic life was not for him and also that America did not have the same appeal as Australia and that neither held his affection like his own native Borderland.

After two years he returned home, and in 1908 he married Madge, daughter of Tom Scott Anderson of Ettrick Shaws and began to earn his living by his pen. He wrote non-stop, in all publishing twenty books of poems and several songs set for solo singing. His routine was after he finished breakfast and read prayers he would sit down with pencil and pad. Usually he started with a couplet, about some thought that had taken his fancy, sometimes he would interrupt his writing with a walk in the garden before returning to his writing. Once the piece was finalised he would write out a copy, never using a typewriter As soon as the poem was printed he would cut it out and paste it in a book and destroy the original, there are very few of his original manuscripts in his original handwriting.

In 1909 he wrote *Whaup O' the Rede* a long riding ballad which expressed his love for his native Borderland. One of his other great loves was horses, with his sporting verses, *Galloping shoes*, *Scattered scarlet*, *Over the grass* and a *Handful of leather* being published in the 1920's. His *Collected Sporting Verse* was published in the early 1930s.

Outback Hall of Fame. Longreach

During World War 1 he accepted a job at a Remount Depot run by the artist G.D. Armour in Wiltshire. Raw horses were transported from Canada to be broken in for use by the British Army, Ogilvie put to good use the skills gained in Australia with the wild buckjumpers. He also worked with Armour and the poet/illustrator combination contributed weekly to *Punch*. This resulted in 115 of his poems being printed in the journal.

Will H Ogilvie never achieved the same recognition in his native Scotland as he did in Australia. He died at his home Kirklea, Ashkirk on 30th January 1963. His ashes were scattered along with wattle leaves from the Bushmen of Australia on The Hill Road to Roberton, where a cairn has now been erected to his memory.

KELSO BRIDGE

THERE is one spot where memory guides
From time to time my restless heart –
A fair, fair spot, where silver tides
Break on grey piers and drift apart
Round pillars spun with water-weed,
Down channels where the foam is whirled;
So beats my love of home, O Tweed!
Against the barriers of the world!
Sunlit or swept by winter's blast
The old bridge stands, a link between
The Abbey's hoar and wrinkled past
And the young elm-bud's waking green;
The nesting rooks above it wheel
From elm to elm on sable wings;
Beneath it, racing round the reel,
The line upon the bent rod sings.
Across the world hope's bridges bear
The wanderer's never-resting feet,
But peace and rest are mingled where
Earth's fairest rivers, mingling, meet.
On pillars twined with water-weed
Your silver tide is ceaseless hurled;
So beats my love of home, O Tweed!
Against the barriers of the world!

Rosemary Payne, Athens.

Rosemary Payne (nee Charters) was born 19th May 1933 in Kelso. Although she always won races at school, it was not until she attended Edinburgh University to read for an MA in general arts that she had her first opportunity to throw the discus. Rosemary became one of Britain's greatest and most durable discus throwers.

In 1958 at the then Empire Games, Rosemary finished 10th with a throw of 34.96 metres. By 1966 she finished 4th in the Commonwealth Games in Kingston, Jamaica and won the gold medal for Scotland in the 1970 Commonwealth Games. In 1972 she represented Great Britain in the women's discus, at the Munich Olympic Games, reaching the final with an excellent 56.50 metres. *(The Munich Games were marred by tragedy when eight Palestinian terrorists from the Black September Group, entered the Olympic village attacked the Israeli team, killing 2 members and taking 9 hostages).* In 1974 she was silver medallist at the Commonwealth Games in New Zealand. She was also a pioneer hammer thrower as well as a good shot putter. In all Rosemary won 11 Scottish titles, 5 British AAA crowns and contested 3 European Championships. She made some 50 GB appearances, despite not making her debut until the age of 30 and she threw over 55 metres several times, which is still difficult for female competitors today.

In 1974 Rosemary retired and was appointed the GB team manager nurturing the talents of athletes such as Steve Cram, Fatima Whitbread, Colin Jackson and Steve Buckley. Returning to competition at Veterans (Masters) level, she lifted 16 world titles and set four world records.

She is now a key member of the Midlands AA Committee helping to bring on new coaches, whilst also playing golf.

Discus thrower Rosemary Payne is the first field athlete to enter the Scottish Borders Sporting Hall of Fame.

Picture Scottish Borders Sporting Hall of Fame.

Sir Matthew Pinsent

b. 1970

Knighted in the 2005 New Years Honours list (following an MBE in 1993 and CBE in 2001) Sir Matthew Pinsent is one of Great Britain's most successful athletes of all time.

Matthew's father was rector of St. Andrew's Church Kelso and Matthew attended Edenside Primary School before going on to Eton College. There he was introduced to the sport of rowing. In 1992, as well as graduating in Geography from St. Catherine's College, Oxford, Matthew was President of the Oxford Rowing Club. That year, at the age of 21 and after an unbeaten season, he with Sir Steve Redgrave, won Gold in the coxless pairs at the Barcelona Olympics. They repeated this success at the Atlanta Olympics in 1996 and their outstanding combination brought them seven World Championship golds. By the Millennium Olympics in Sydney, Matthew and Stephen teamed up with James Cracknell and Tim Foster in a coxless four, to win Steve's *third* Olympic gold medal.

After the Sydney Olympics, Matthew formed a seemingly invincible coxless pairs partnership with James Cracknell MBE. Undefeated through 2001, they defended their coxed pairs title at the 2002 World Championships in Seville, beating an experienced Australian crew and breaking the world record by 4 seconds.

On Saturday 21st August 2004 at the Athens Olympics, Matthew became one of only 5 athletes to win *four* consecutive Olympic gold medals when he led Great Britain to success in the coxless fours. He retired from competitive rowing in 2004.

Achievements:

Olympic Games	
1992	Gold - Barcelona, Coxless Pair
1996	Gold - Atlanta, Coxless Pair
2000	Gold - Sydney, Coxless Four
2000	Flag bearer - Sydney, Team GB
2004	Gold - Athens, Coxless Four

World Championships	
1991	Gold – Vienna, Coxless Pair
1993	Gold – Roudnice, Coxless Pair
1994	Gold – Indianapolis, Coxless Pair
1995	Gold – Tampere, Coxless Pair
1997	Gold – Lac d'Aiguebelette, Coxless Four
1998	Gold – Cologne, Coxless Four
1999	Gold – St Catherine's, Coxless Four
2001	Gold – Lucerne, Coxed Pair
2001	Gold – Lucerne, Coxless Pair
2002	Gold – Seville, Coxless Pair

Thomas Pringle

1789-1834

Thomas Pringle from Poetical Works of Thomas Pringle

Thomas was born the third of five children to Robert Pringle and Katherine Heatlie who farmed at Blakelaw. As a baby he was dropped and dislocated his hip, laming him for life. Their church was the Anti-Burger (secession) congregation in Morebattle. When Thomas was six, his mother died and is buried in Linton kirkyard. His father re-married to Beatrice Scott.

Thomas attended Kelso Grammar School and in 1803 went to Edinburgh University, attending lectures on chemistry, logic and metaphysics. He was particularly interested in the travels of Mungo Park. He started a weekly club for literary criticism and wrote poetry attracting the friendship of Sir Walter Scott. After he became employed as a clerk in the Records Office, he wrote articles for periodicals and became joint editor of the *Edinburgh Monthly Magazine*. After quarrelling with John Blackwood, he became joint editor to the *Edinburgh Star* (now called *Constable's*) and published *Autumnal Excursion and other poems* in 1818.

In February 1820 (under a government scheme to create settlements in South Africa) Thomas, his father, brothers, 3 farm servants, 6 women and 6 children, set sail in 'The Brilliant', anchoring in Simons Bay on 30th April. On 6th June, Thomas helped to lay the foundation stone of the first house of the new town of Port Elizabeth.

A large party of settlers, including the Pringles made their way to the upper valley of the Baviaans River to Glen Lynden. The Pringles called their farm 'Eildon'. Everything had to be created from scratch for the settlers and Thomas' carpentry skills were much in demand. The communal bread oven he created from a termite's nest, was in use for several years and the Scotch plough they had brought from home only needed one man and two oxen, unlike the Dutch plough which needed up to four men and 12 oxen. He loathed all aspects of the slave trade and learned Dutch so that he could help the Hottentots.

In 1822, Thomas left his brother at the farm and was made sub-librarian in the Government Library in Cape Town, at a salary of £75 a year. He joined fellow-journalist and friend John Fairbairn and opened a school. He also started a literary society, a publication called the *South African Journal* and edited the *South African Commercial Advertiser*.

Thomas collected evidence of abuses in the administration led by Lord Charles Somerset and of the ill-treatment of the Hottentots. Lord Charles viewed a free press as a crime and liberal leanings an offence and closed the school, sealed the presses and ordered local men to quit the literary society. Pringle travelled around the Colony recording evidence of abuse which he passed to the Commissioners of Enquiry in London and in 1828 the Hottentots were given equal rights.

Thomas' position became untenable. He visited the family in Glen Lynden and found the settlement prospering, numbers growing, flocks increasing and new houses built. In later years, the settlement would incorporate the township of Kelso. Before leaving the Cape, Thomas wrote an article on the slave question in the *New Monthly Review* which brought him to the notice of Wilberforce, Buxton and Zachary Macaulay and arrived back in London on 7th July 1826, with debts of £1,000 (thanks largely to the vindictiveness of Lord Charles Somerset)

From 1827 he worked as Secretary to the Anti-Slavery Society, wrote the memoirs of Dr Alexander Waugh and supplied material for Thompson's *Travels in South Africa* and offered his services to the Government to return to South Africa in connection with measures for the protection of slaves.

In 1833, shortly before the death of Wilberforce, all slaves in British possessions were emancipated and the Act of Abolition was finally signed on 27th June 1834.

On 5th December 1834 Thomas Pringle died from tuberculosis and is buried in Bunhill Fields Cemetary in London. In 1951, the Scottish Settlers Memorial Church was built on the Eildon Farm (still farmed by the fifth generation of Pringles). In 1970 Thomas' remains were re-interred in this Church.

Sir William Purves, CBE, DSO

b. 1931

William Purves was born in December 1931 at Kersquarter, Kelso where his father was tenant farmer until 1932. The family then moved to Bedrule, Hawick where his mother resumed her career as a schoolteacher. In 1942 the family moved to Ednam, Kelso when his mother was appointed Headmistress of the local school.

Sir William Purves

William (Willie) was educated at Kelso High School and having attained a Higher Leaving Certificate in 1948 he became an apprentice at a salary of £48 per annum in the National Bank of Scotland Kelso, (later National Commercial Bank, later Royal Bank of Scotland). His banking career was interrupted by his call up for National Service where he was badged into the Black Watch and trained at Fort George. He was then sent to Eaton Hall, Chester, as an Officer Cadet before being Commissioned into the King's Own Scottish Borderers which Regiment he joined in Hong Kong in early 1951. Almost immediately the Regiment was sent to Korea to replace the Argyll and Sutherland Highlanders in the United Nations Forces. The Regiment saw considerable action and in November 1951 Purves was awarded the Distinguished Service Order for gallantry in the field at the age of 19. (No other National Service officer was awarded this high honour).

On demobilisation Willie returned to the National Bank at 10, The Square where he firstly became Ledger Clerk and subsequently Teller. He was then invited to transfer to Head Office Edinburgh but since the offered salary would not cover the cost of his digs, he resigned in 1954. After interviews with a number of foreign banks, he joined The Hongkong and Shanghai Banking Corporation later that year.

So commenced a career of 44 years with what is now HSBC Holdings plc, all but 40 of which were worked mainly in the Far East, with periodic leaves spent happily in the Borders. He married Diana Richardson in 1959 in Singapore, who bore him two daughters and two sons. They separated in 1988 and Purves married Rebecca Lewellen the following year.

Purves worked his way up in what was locally called, the Hongkong Bank, before being appointed Chief Executive in 1986 and Group Chairman at the end of the same year. The Bank was growing fast as the economies of many Asian countries developed but was clearly under represented in Europe. Purves and his colleagues therefore set about the search for a partner of some size. In 1983 they were prevented by the Monopolies Commission from taking over the Royal Bank of Scotland, which could well have brought the combined Head Office to Edinburgh but when Midland Bank, one of the largest clearers, got into trouble in 1985 the opportunity to take a minority stake of 14.9% arose. Merger discussions followed over some years until a full takeover was proposed by HSBC in 1991. Despite the threatened intervention of Lloyds Bank, opposition from the Bank of England, difficulties with other Regulators and worries in China, Purves pushed ahead and gained control of Midland in July 1992. This resulted in him having to leave his beloved Hong Kong in October 1993 and take up residence in London.

While in Hong Kong Purves held office in a number of charitable and sporting organisations and was a member of The Executive Council – Hong Kong's highest Governing Body. He was Chairman of the Royal Hong Kong Jockey Club and of the Hong Kong Sports Development Authority and Treasurer of the University of Hong Kong. He was appointed a Commander of the British Empire for services to Hong Kong in 1989 and was Knighted by Her Majesty in 1993 for services to Banking and Hong Kong. In 2001 he was awarded the Grand Bauhinia Order, the highest order bestowed by the Hong Kong Special Autonomous Region.

After his transfer to London he was appointed a Non-Exec Director of Shell Transport and Trading and became a Trustee of the Imperial War Museum (subsequently Deputy Chairman) and of Charterhouse in the City. He retired in 1998 from all offices in the HSBC Group, including Chairman of Midland Bank and British Bank of the Middle East.

After retirement, he became a non-executive director of Alstom SA, Chairman of Hakluyt & Company and non-executive Director of a number of non-quoted companies. For a time he was seconded to the committee of the Scottish Rugby Union and became a Trustee of the National Museums of Scotland and more recently Vice President of the National Trust for Scotland. In 2004/5 he was Master of the Guild of International Bankers. He was honoured by receiving honorary degrees from nine universities in Hong Kong and the United Kingdom.

Although now living in London and North Oxfordshire Purves continues to take a close interest in developments in the Borders. His sport is Rugby Union and he loves gardening.

Banking Career

The National Bank of Scotland, Kelso	
1948	Apprenticeship
1953	Ledger Clerk and Teller
The Hongkong and Shanghai Banking Corporation	
1954	Hamburg Office
1955	Hong Kong main office
1957	Johore Bahru, Malaysia
1958	Singapore
1959-62	Ceylon (now Sri Lanka)
1963	Hong Kong main office
1964-65	Tokyo, Japan
1966-67	Hong Kong main office
1968	Head of Securities and Investments, Hong Kong
1969-73	Chief Accountant, Hong Kong
1974-75	Manager, Tokyo, Japan
1976	London office
1977-78	Assistant General Manager Overseas Operations, Head Office, Hong Kong
1979-82	General Manager International
1982-84	Executive Director Banking, Head Office, Hong Kong
1984-86	Deputy Chairman, Head Office, Hong Kong
1986	Chief Executive, Head Office, Hong Kong
HSBC Holdings plc	
1987-98	Group Chairman also Chairman Midland Bank 1993-98

Ladyrig

railways allowed manures and drainage tiles to be brought in cheaply and bulky crops like potatoes (previously grown only for local use) could now be profitably increased. Many farmers came to Ladyrig to learn from James Roberton, among them Herr Schiffert of Hamburg, Count de Courcy of Paris and a Mr la Noski from Odessa. James Roberton set up scientific trials to gauge the exact effect of weeds on a wheat crop. He was the first Secretary of the Kelso Analytical and Testing Association (set up in 1859) and the Tweedside Agricultural Museum Society (set up in 1841). In 1876 he wrote *The History of a Farm* about Soursides.

Clifton

Ladyrig, between Heiton and the Bowmont Forest, was farmed by the ROBERTON family for more than 200 years from 1778. At that time the only fertiliser was the manure produced by beasts on the farm; lime was seldom applied; there were no artificial animal foodstuffs; drainage was poor or non-existent and the land was still divided into the 'infield' and the poor grazing of the 'outfield'. From 1799, the Robertons carried out cross-draining of the boggy areas, deepened ditches and installed a water-wheel. From 1818, the application of bone meal began and this, combined with better drainage, saw a doubling in weight of crops like turnips.

JAMES ROBERTON took the fourth lease (1837-72). Better drainage, plus the use of bone meal and guano, brought wet soils under cultivation with spring wheat and barley, while sterile moor was able to produce fine crops of turnips. The

Frogden

Kelso farmers were at the forefront of the agricultural revolution which began in the 18th century. In the 1760s, William Dawson of Frogden was the first in the area to use the drill system for turnips and reclaimed, drained and fertilized the land. In January 1813 the Border Agricultural Society was formed, holding its first show in September in the Knowes and offered £50 to Mr Robert Glaister of Wooler to set up a veterinary practice in Kelso. In 1852, Kelso Farmers Club took part in a scientific trial of different manures. In the latter half of the 19th century, Robert Elliot of Clifton Park experimented using the 'ley' system of crop rotation.

Mrs Margaret Robertson of Shedden Park

1786-1872

Gates at Shedden Park

In 1818 Ednam House was bought by John Robertson, a successful merchant in London but originally from Kelso. (His brother-in-law ran the Ednam brewery.) His wife Margaret was born in Berwick and her grandfather was formerly minister of Bedrule, so she too had local connections. They had been married for ten years when they decided to settle in Kelso. In 1842 John died, but his widow continued to live in Ednam House until her death. Well known for her many charitable works in the town, Mrs Robertson regularly gave money to the Inspector of the Poor to help destitute people in Kelso. She took a great interest in the Ragged School and left it an annuity in her will. She contributed much of the cost of the rebuilding of St Andrews Episcopal church in 1869, by the famous architect Robert Rowand Anderson.

However, her greatest gift to the town was undoubtedly Shedden Park. In October 1850, on learning of the untimely death of her favourite nephew Robert Shedden, she decided to preserve his memory, by giving to the people of Kelso a public park to be named in his honour. Two fields were purchased next to the Coldstream Road for £1200 - a lot of money in those days - and Mrs Robertson gave a further £500 to lay paths, plant trees and shrubs and enclose the park with railings. She later donated two cannons from Shedden's ship, which stood in front of the Keeper's Lodge; and she also gave to the trustees some houses in Rose Lane whose rents would provide income to run the park.

Such was the gratitude of the people of Kelso that a fund was started to raise a memorial arch at the entrance to Shedden Park in honour of Mrs Robertson. The park was officially inaugurated in October 1851 with a grand procession, a ball and a bonfire in the Square.

The Schooner Nancy Dawson

Who was Robert Shedden?

Robert Shedden was Mrs Robertson's nephew. His family were regular visitors to Kelso. He had a successful career in the Navy rising to the rank of Lieutenant Commander. In 1848 he set sail from Leith in a schooner, the *Nancy Dawson*, which he had equipped from his own resources. He intended to go round the world collecting information for the Geographical Society, and also to help in the search for Sir John Franklin. In 1845 Franklin, a famous Arctic explorer had set off with two ships to try to find a route around northern Canada. His ships disappeared without trace in the polar ice and by 1848 a full scale search was under way to try to find him and his men.

In 1849 Robert Shedden in the *Nancy Dawson* joined two naval vessels in searching the area between the Behring Straits and the Mackenzie River. Shedden sailed further to the north-east of the Straits than any ship before. However, in September, with a mutinous crew, worn down with illness and with the ice closing in, Shedden was forced to turn back. His ship headed for Mazatlan in Mexico where he died in November aged only 28 years.

Extract from the terms of the Trust for Shedden Park

That the subjects shall be kept used and maintained in all time coming, as a public promenade or playground, in which the inhabitants of Kelso shall be entitled to practise and enjoy all lawful, healthful and commendable sports, recreations and amusements.

Extract from Local Newspaper October 18th 1850

(Mrs Robertson's) acts of public and private charity have long been known in Kelso and .. on a visit of the Church Commissioners in 1837, one of the gentlemen made enquiry who Mrs Robertson was, as in almost every house he had visited he heard the name of this benevolent lady on the lips of rich and poor...... It is therefore with no small pride we draw attention to the handsome boon Mrs Robertson has bestowed on the town of Kelso, by the presentation of a piece of ground to be set apart for public games and recreation..... It is an act of princely benevolence for which the present and many a coming generation cannot be too grateful.

John Robson

John Robson

I was born in Kelso on the 31st of January 1957. The family lived in Roxburgh Street which was fantastic for an active child as I had The Cobby and Croft Park on my doorstep. I attended Kelso Primary and High Schools where my main sport was rugby rather than athletics, but the school held an annual cross country race where I discovered I had a gift for distance running. I ran locally up to aged sixteen when I joined Edinburgh Southern Harriers competing for them in The British League.

My International career took off when I competed for Great Britain in a dual meet at Crystal Palace, London against West Germany in 1977 where I broke four minutes for the mile aged twenty. I then was a regular for The Scottish National and Great Britain team for nine years competing in three Commonwealth Games, two European Championships, and numerous World Cross Country Championships. During my career I was ranked fourth in the world for the 1500 metres in 1978 and 1979, won a Commonwealth Games bronze Medal in 1978 in Edmonton Canada. Moreover I won a bronze medal

in 1979 Euro indoor 1500m in Vienna Austria. I currently still hold the Scottish 1500m and 3000m records, the 1500m has stood for 29 years. Throughout my career I was coached by the late John Lauder who ran a bookmaking business in Kelso. Most of my training was done locally in The Floors Estate and Shedden Park.

I live with my family, wife Sandra and son Steven on The Hendersyde Estate and have run a small business from home as a remedial massage therapist for nearly ten years. I also work with the local rugby team tending to their numerous injuries during the season.

I still run, but only for fitness now and stopped competing in 1999 when aged 42. I love training around Kelso and watching the seasons changing in the fantastic scenery.

John Robson winning

1 mile ("Emsley Carr" Trophy)

Robson	3:55.83 (55.8)
Williamson	3:56.40 (56.4)
Foster	3:57.37 (57.4)
Cram	3:57.42 (57.4)
Hutchings	3:57.83 (57.8)
Masback	3:58.04 (58.0)
Hartel	4:00.04 (00.0)
Emson	4:00.48 (00.5)
Smedley	4:00.85 (00.9)
Maplestone	4:00.92 (00.9)
Kipkurgat	4:03.11 (03.1)
Chimes	4:12.51 (12.5)
Leach	4:19.95 (20.0)

Sir Walter Scott

1771-1832

The roots of Sir Walter Scott were very much implanted in Kelso. Although he was born in Edinburgh in 1771, Sir Walter Scott spent much of his childhood in or near Kelso. His great - grandfather Walter "Beardie" Scott held land in Kelso, including a house on the corner of Simon Square. His grandfather was Robert Scott of Sandyknowe Farm, his uncle Captain Robert Scott of Rosebank House and his Aunt Jenny who lived at the Garden House – now Waverley Lodge.

Rosebank

One of his main Kelso inspirations was Lancelot Whale – a teacher at Kelso Grammar School, who tutored him in the classics. Whale, however was not keen on "profane" English or Scottish literature which the young Scott enjoyed and would read at night by firelight. A solution was *"a respectable subscription library, a circulating library of ancient standing, and some private bookshelves"* in Kelso. His favourite book was Bishop Percy's *Reliques of Ancient Poetry*, which he recalls reading for the first time under a large tree in Aunt Jenny's garden.

It was at Kelso Grammar School that Scott first encountered James Ballantyne, who was later to become his business partner and printer of his books. Scott went on to study law at Edinburgh University and was admitted to the Faculty of Advocates. During a later visit to Rosebank, Ballantyne asked Scott to supply an article on some legal question of the day for the Kelso Mail of which Ballantyne was the printer and editor. Scott on delivering the article to the printing office asked why they *did not try to get a little booksellers work, to keep his types in play during the rest of the week*. From that remark a partnership was borne that would lead even in adversity to a lifelong friendship.

Ballantyne printed *Apology for Tales of Terror* and Scott was delighted with the result. Scott had spent many years on a labour of love, he had travelled around the Borders gathering old Border ballads. These were collected into two volumes and printed by Ballantyne. In early 1802 the *Minstrelsy of the Scottish Border* was printed in Kelso. Owing to the success of this collection, Ballantyne moved his business to Edinburgh and became Scott's business partner and lifelong friend.

Bust at Waverley Lodge

The *Minstrelsy of the Scottish Border* was Scott's first major success and he went on to become one of the most successful and prolific Scottish writers.

Kelso can boast many buildings that were associated with Sir Walter Scott.

Apology for Tales of Terror - picture Ballantyne Press

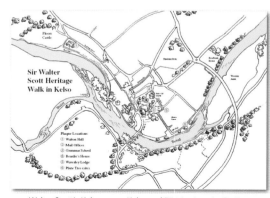

Walter Scott's Kelso map – Kelso and District Amenity Society

Georgiana Margaret Solomon

1844-1933

Born in Haymount Kelso to an unsuccessful 'gentleman farmer' George Thomson and Margaret Scott from Melrose. Georgiana had to earn her living as a teacher. Her parents had connections with the Rev. Andrew Murray (Dutch Reformed Church) in Cape Town. He had been active in women's education and planned to establish a school, the Good Hope Seminary, for the higher education of girls in Cape Town. In 1873, Georgiana was invited to become lady principal.

Georgiana met and married Saul Solomon (1817-1892) – she was 29 and he 56. He was proprietor of the *Cape Argus*, a member of the legislative assembly for Cape Town and a noted liberal and philanthropist. Solomon emphasised *racial equality* between black and white, where other liberals pressed for legal and constitutional equality. Through the Solomon extended family, Georgiana became a member of a circle of educated, enlightened and politically active women at the Cape (including Olive Shreiner author of *Story of an African Farm*). A deeply committed Christian, Georgiana was active in the temperance and purity movements. In 1888, Saul's health broke down following the death by drowning of their elder daughter and the family returned to Britain. Saul died in 1892. Georgiana wrote a book of poems *Echo of Two little Voices*.

Now resident in England, Georgiana revisited South Africa and was involved in the women's suffrage movement, which emerged there in 1902 at the end of the South African War. It was non-militant taking the form of 'welfare feminism'. She collaborated with General Louis Botha's wife Annie, to form the Suid-Afrikaanse Vrouefederasie (SAVF) which embraced reconciliation between Boers and British and aided Boer families devastated by the War. Back in England she joined the Women's Social and Political Union and in 1909 led a deputation to the House of Commons, but was unable to meet Prime Minister Asquith.

Haymount

On 18th November 1910, she was brutally assaulted by the police during a further deputation to the Commons, which left her invalided for a while. In March 1912 she and daughter Daisy served one month's imprisonment in Holloway gaol, for breaking 7 small windows in the office of Black Rod at the House of Lords. She remained active in the purity movement, a member of the Women's Freedom League and was a vice-president of the Free Church League for Women's Suffrage as well as Honorary president of the SAVF.

She was appalled by the Act of Union in South Africa, which failed to extend suffrage to black men. She lobbied against the 1913 Land Act which deprived Africans of the right to own land in South Africa. She believed that it was England which was promoting the colour bar, stultifying development and increasing the 'miseries and perils' of black women. Looked after by Daisy, she died in Eastbourne aged 88.

Jane Stoddart

1863-1944

Born at 29 Horse Market, Kelso on 2nd November 1863, Jane Thompson Stoddart became an author and a journalist. Jane attended the Kelso Ladies College at Maitland House in Forestfield in Kelso. Her later autobiography entitled *My Harvest of the Years* recounted her experience at her Kelso school giving a fascinating description of the teachers and her life at the school as a boarder.

At that time the Rev. William Robertson Nicoll (later to become Sir William Robertson Nicoll CH) was the Free Church minister in Kelso, and he was to greatly influence her life.

She became a pupil teacher at Bruntsfield, Edinburgh where she enthusiastically observed the first Midlothian campaign by William Gladstone. In 1881 she went to Hanover to teach and learn German, translating Richard Rothe's *Stille Stunden* in 1888.

Moving back to Great Britain she taught at Durdham Down, Clifton for three years, where she wrote her only fiction *A Door of Hope* (1886) and *In Cheviots Glens* (1887).

In 1890 she became a full-time journalist, working as assistant editor of *The British Weekly*, of which Nicoll was the editor. This was at that time the chief London nonconformist paper. At a time when the interview was becoming a prominent feature of British weeklies, she became the paper's chief interviewer, publishing many of her interviews under the byline *Lorna*. She also became assistant editor of *Woman at Home*, an illustrated magazine intended as a *Strand*

Maitland House, Forestfield

Magazine for women, and subtitled 'Annie S. Swan's Magazine', with the Scottish novelist being chief contributor.

Stoddart maintained a steady stream of publications including the biographies *The Life of Empress Eugenie* (1906) and *The Girlhood of Mary Queen of Scotts* (1908). Her *The New Testament in Life and Literature* was a substantial work.

Introducing readers to a wide, and for the time, varied sources, her *New Socialism: an Impartial Inquiry* was a valuable work. After World War One she published *The Case against Spiritualism* (1919) and other works including her aforementioned autobiography in 1938.

CHAPTER ONE

Early Years in Kelso

The Town of Two Rivers . Scenes of Beauty . Safe Roads . The Old Castle . My First School . A Welsh Headmistress . Books and Newspapers . Free Church Life . Dr. Horatius Bonar . Poet and Friend

THE town of Kelso, in Roxburghshire, where I was born on All Souls' Day, 1863, was described by Sir Walter Scott, in his fragment of autobiography, as the most beautiful if not the most romantic village in Scotland. Memory shows me a clean and stately town, with five thousand inhabitants and ten churches. The central Square has been compared by H. V. Morton to the noble *place* he has seen in old-world Continental cities. The Town Hall, the chief hotel, the most important shops, came within or near its boundaries.

From a friend's house overlooking the Square we children watched the weekly market, the crowds assembled for the annual race-meeting, and the bonfires lit for celebrations in the Duke of Roxburghe's family. Five streets, radiating from this centre, were corridors to the country. We had no organised school games, but young people learned early the habit of walking for pleasure. The legend-haunted rivers Tweed and Teviot, the mouldering

9

10   My Harvest of the Years

stones of Kelso Abbey, awakened in sensitive minds that "intense impression of reverence" of which Sir Walter wrote, "which at times made my heart feel too big for its bosom."

The road to Ednam, birthplace of James Thomson, the poet of *The Seasons*, was familiar ground when I was eight or nine. It was here that my father told me the story of Macbeth as an introduction to Shakespeare, and of Oliver Twist as my earliest taste of Dickens. I could point out long afterwards the dark clump of trees which he compared to Birnam Wood that came to Dunsinane. As the eldest of five, I was soon leading my own small company for walks and picnics. Except on the bridge and near the station, there was little traffic and no need for special vigilance. 'Twas sixty years since, and a good world for children. Road accidents were almost unknown.

The first glimpse of the Cheviot slopes, as we walked towards Yetholm, was welcome as the sight of the Downs to travellers on the Brighton Railway. We were emerging from the hollow land, with its relaxing air and steamy heat. Another hour would bring us to the foot of the hills. Pedestrians kept the middle of the highway, their ears attentive for the rare sound of a doctor's gig, a tradesman's van, or the postman's cart for Yetholm. Not less quiet, as I remember, was the road to Berwick, which ran

Early Days in Kelso   11

parallel with the Tweed, and kept the north bank of the stream. One of our joys was the crossing by "Willie's boat" at the ferry opposite Sprouston. We were nearer the frontiers of England.

The best walk was to Roxburgh Castle, whose green mounds overhang the Teviot. Sir Walter mentions its "distant vestiges" along with the modern stateliness of its neighbour, Floors Castle, the home of the Roxburghes, whose magnificent gardens were sometimes opened to the public. Children "paced" their dyed eggs at Easter among the ancient ruins, gathered primroses in the rich woodland soil of Daniel's Den, and re-enacted the wars of Bruce in games of hide-and-seek. Scots and English fought through centuries for the possession of this stronghold.

That wisest of counsellors, W. Robertson Nicoll, used to say that there is no better equipment for life than a sound, plain education. He would have agreed with Kim's Lama that "education is greatest blessing if of best sorts, otherwise no earthly use." I was fortunate in my first teacher, Miss Eliza Williams, a Welsh lady, who had established a successful school on the outskirts of the town. Well-known families in three counties entrusted their daughters to her care. Kelso parents considered themselves happy if their girls could be received as day pupils among the boarders at Maitland House.

First three pages of My Harvest of the Years

Thomas Tod Stoddart

1810-1880

Thomas Tod Stoddart was born in Edinburgh on 14th February 1810. He was one of seven children of Captain (later Admiral) Pringle Stoddart and Frances Sprot. After Edinburgh High School, Thomas went to the University of Edinburgh, at the age of 15, to read law. In 1833 he was admitted to the Faculty of Advocates, but never practised. Thomas had developed a passion for angling and the art of angling – a passion that had been passed down from his father, and it was angling that became his chief occupation.

Thomas Tod Stoddart was known as an expert angler and fly-maker and he formed friendships with renowned anglers such as Rob Kerss of the Trows. He began writing on the subject of angling and his papers on *"The Art of Angling"* were published in Chambers's Journal. In 1835 these were published in book form which was the first treatise of its kind in Scotland. A new and enlarged edition followed a year later and *Angling Reminiscences* in 1837. Ten years later *The Angler's Companion to the Rivers and Lochs of Scotland* was published. His fourth and last book on angling was *An Angler's Rambles and Angling Songs* which consisted of fascinating reminiscences interspersed with verse. From childhood, Stoddart loved writing verse and his poetry received a prize for *"idolatry"* at the age of 16. His first printed verses were entitled "An Address to the Scottish Thistle" which appeared in the short-lived publication *Lapsus Linguœ*. Stoddart published volumes of verse including *"Songs of the Seasons"*, *"Angling Songs"* and *"The Death-Wake or Lunacy, a necromaunt in three chimeras"*. He had many friends in the literary world including James Hogg, the Ettrick Shepherd, who was also a fishing companion.

In April 1836 Thomas married Elizabeth (Bessie) MacGregor of Contin, Ross-shire and the following year the couple moved to Kelso, eventually setting up home at Bellevue Cottage. He found Kelso a place congenial to his tastes and for forty-three years it was his home. He was president

Fisherman on the Tweed

and secretary of Teviotdale Angling Club and he was also president of the Kelso Angling Club. Thomas Tod Stoddart died in Kelso on 21 November 1880 and is buried at Rosebank Cemetery beside his wife who died in 1886 and their daughter who died in 1911. His two sons Pringle and John lived in New Zealand. During his funeral the bell of the Town Hall was tolled at intervals of a minute.

IN PRAISE OF TWEED

Let ither anglers chuse their ain,
And ither waters tak' the lead;
O'Hielan' streams we covet nane,
But gie to us the bonnie Tweed!
And gie to us the cheerfu' burn
That steals into its valley fair –
The streamlets that at ilka turn
Sau saftly meet an mingle there.

The lanesome Talla and the Lyne,
An' Manor wi' its mountain rills,
An' Etterick, whose waters twine
We' Yarrow frae the Forest hills;
An' Gala too, and Teviot bright,
An' mony a stream o' playfu' speed;
Their kindred valleys a' unite
Amang the braes o' bonnie Tweed.

There's no a hole abune the Crook,
Nor stane nor gentle swirl aneath,
Nor drumlie rill nor faery brook,
That daunders thro' the flowery heath,
But ye may fin' a subtle troot,
A'gleamin' ower wi' starn an' bead.
An' mony a sawmon sooms about
Below the bields o' bonnie Tweed.

Frae Holylee to Clovenford,
A chancier bit ye canna hae
So gin ye tak' an angler's word,
Ye'd through the whins an' ower the brae.
An' work awa' wi' cunnin' hand
Yer birzy hackles, black and reid;
The saft sough o' a slender wand
Is meetest music for the Tweed!

Thomas Tod Stoddart

From BUCHAN, J
The Northern Muse: An anthology of Scots Vernacular Poetry

Tait Hall and the Tait Family

Built 1935

Tait Hall, Kelso picture courtesy Friends of Kelso Museum.

On February 7th 1930, Provost Wight was able to announce a most generous legacy to the town of Kelso - £10,000 left by William Edgar Tait for the purpose of the construction of a hall "suitable for the needs of the community".

William Tait belonged to a leading Kelso family. His grandfather, Captain James Tait who belonged to an old Berwickshire family from Langrigg in Berwickshire had been involved in the Indian trade. He bought Edenside House in Kelso and his only son James was born there in 1816. James Tait played a leading part in the life of the town throughout his life, as a lawyer, agent for the National Bank and founder of the law firm which still bears his name. He was also heavily engaged in public business, playing a leading part in the development of what would become Kelso Town Council. (Formerly the Town had been run by Stentmasters appointed by the Duke.) James Tait had six sons and one daughter. His fourth son David followed his father into the family law firm, as

well as being involved with the Town Council. Several of the sons seem to have left Kelso and gone abroad to work. We know that Stormont Tait became a wine merchant in Oporto and John Tait went out to Perak in modern Malaysia.

William Edgar, the third son and the benefactor of the Tait Hall went out to New Zealand, where he was first of all a partner in a timber business. He later became the owner of the Woodlands Canning Factory near Invercargill. The business prospered and he sold it shortly after the First World War and retired. He seems to have returned to Scotland for the family grave records that he died in Edinburgh in January 1930, aged 75, the last of the brothers to die.

Arthur Middlemas picture courtesy Kelso and District Amenity Society.

ARTHUR MIDDLEMAS
While the lawyers sorted out the transfer of the money from New Zealand, another problem was solved by the generosity of Arthur Middlemas, proprietor of the Aerated Water Factory which used to be in Roxburgh Street. He had served for many years on the Town Council including a spell as Provost. He gifted to the town the land next to

Painting of original colour scheme, picture courtesy Friends of Kelso Museum.

his property at Charlesfield, Edenside Road as a site for the new hall. He retired soon after due to ill health and sadly died before the hall was completed.

The new Tait Hall was completed by 1935 and was officially opened on Wednesday September 25th, by Miss Margaret Tait of Edenside House, the last surviving member of the family. The occasion was marked by a civic luncheon with about 200 guests. In his address to Miss Tait Provost Scott said

"The name of Tait has the honourable distinction of being associated with Kelso for nearly 120 years and this munificent gift will carry on your honoured name to a generation yet unborn. There they stand in spirit, clasping hand in hand, William Edgar Tait and Arthur Middlemas, rejoicing with us today on the completion of this fine edifice which will be a lasting memorial of their love and devotion for their native town."

George Taylor

George Taylor was born at Hownam Grange in 1803. He was the son of a shepherd, Andrew Taylor, who worked on several farms including Attonburn, Ladyrig, Crailing Tofts and Wester Wooden. George describes moving from place to place and the work conditions of the time in his memoirs, *From Kelso to Kalamazoo*. These have now been published as a book edited by Margaret Jeary and Mark Mulhern.

He became the gardener at Ormiston Farm in the 1830s and eventually became manager of a market garden in Forestfield, Kelso. Mrs Robertson of Ednam House, who donated Shedden Park to Kelso, asked him to plant the trees round the park.

In his memoir he describes events such as an election in Jedburgh where Sir Walter Scott was present, his first train journey, the farmer who told his workers they would not be re-hired if they bought newspapers, the Teviot freezing over at Kalemouth Bridge in the winter of 1836/37 and retrieving the body of a young man from Nisbet who fell through the ice.

He used to walk all the way from Eckford to Edinburgh, setting off at 2am and arriving at 4pm, saving the coach fare of ten shillings to spend the money on books. He records his first journey on a train when he went to Ayr and on his travels there he met an old lady who was the widow of Thomas Goldie who was, she said, the original Tam O'Shanter. He supported the Temperance Society and recalls that he once saw three drunken men riding into Kelso Square, all ministers of the church!

In 1855, he took his family to Kalamazoo, Michigan, where he became a gardener and nurseryman. When settled in Kalamazoo, he soon established a successful business supplying plants and hedging. He became an award-winning horticulturalist and was responsible for the introduction of the cultivation of celery to the USA. Kalamazoo became known as "Celery City".

In spite of nearly sinking on the first voyage to America, he came back on visits to Scotland twice, all described in his memoir. As well as crossing the Atlantic five times, he went to Dublin and travelled widely by rail visiting places in Scotland, England (he visited the Great Exhibition and Crystal Palace) and America, including the Niagara Falls. He saw the burning embers of Chicago after the great fire in 1871.

He lived through the Napoleonic Wars, the cholera epidemic, the potato blight, the coming of the railways and the American Civil War and the abolition of slavery.

When he was an old man he began to write down his memories. By then he had outlived four wives, two of whom died in childbirth. He also lost three babies at birth, his son drowned aged 19 and his daughter died of TB.

George Taylor died in 1891, leaving this wonderful memoir of local and social history.

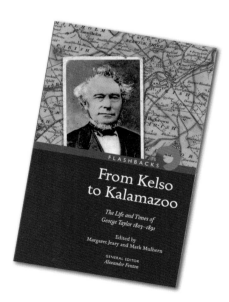

James Thomson

1700-1748

James Thomson
picture courtesy of SCRAN

Plaque on Monument

Thomson Monument

James Thomson was born in Ednam, where his father Thomas had been minister since 1692 and his grandfather had worked as gardener to the local laird, Mr Edmonstone. His mother Beatrix Trotter, from Fogo near Duns, was related to the Humes. James, their fourth child, was born on 11th September 1700. Soon after this the Reverend Thomson and his family moved to Southdean where five more children were born.

James Thomson attended Jedburgh Grammar School, where we are told he was "far from appearing to possess a sprightly genius". However about this time he began to write poetry, encouraged by Robert Riccaltoun, a local farmer, poet and future minister. In 1715 Thomson entered Edinburgh University where he continued to write poetry. The following year his father died, allegedly while exorcising a ghost. James started an Arts degree then changed to Divinity, but in 1725 after a quarrel with his professor, he decided to quit his studies and go to London to seek his fortune.

At first Thomson found work as a tutor to a noble family, but soon he began to make his mark as a poet. His first major work *Winter* was published in 1726 and soon ran into a second edition. *Spring* and *Summer* soon followed, and in 1830 the first collected edition of *The Seasons* including *Autumn* was published. As well as poetry, he wrote a number of plays and in 1740 he collaborated with another writer, Malloch and the composer Thomas Arne, on a masque called *Alfred*, which included the work he is best remembered for today - *Rule Britannia*.

However, in Thomson's own day it was *The Seasons* which was regarded as his masterpiece. His poems extolling the beauty of nature are credited with laying the foundations of the Romantic movement, inspiring poets like Wordsworth and artists like Turner. Before Robert Burns came on the scene, Thomson was regarded as Scotland's leading poet and Burns himself visited the Thomson monument and wrote a poem in his honour. *The Seasons* was translated into German and later became the basis for Haydn's famous oratorio.

James Thomson died on August 27th 1748 after catching a chill while boating, and is buried in Richmond where he had lived for some years.

Lines From Spring

The blackbird whistles from the thorny brake,
The mellow bullfinch answers from the grove;
Nor are the linnets, o'er the flowering furze
Poured out profusely, silent. Joined to these
Innumerous songsters, in the freshening shade
Of new-sprung leaves, their modulations mix
Mellifluous. The jay, the rook, the daw,
And each harsh pipe, discordant heard alone,
Aid the full concert; while the stock-dove breathes
A melancholy murmur through the whole.

Opening lines from Rule Britannia

When Britain first, at Heaven's command,
Arose from out the azure main,
This was the charter of the land,
And guardian angels sung this strain -
Rule Britannia, rule the waves;
Britons never will be slaves.

John Thomson – Composer

John Thomson was born in Sprouston on 28th October 1805, the son of the minister the Rev. Doctor Andrew Thomson and his wife Jane Carmichael. Andrew Thomson was himself an amateur musician who composed church music. After he moved to St George's Edinburgh he worked with choir master R. A. Smith to improve church music and no doubt this background would have influenced the young John Thomson's musical talents.

However, it was as a composer in the romantic movement that John Thomson would make his mark. This was the time when the works of Burns, Scott and Byron were making Scotland famous in Europe and several composers such as Beethoven wrote arrangements of Scottish songs. Thomson too made arrangements of Scottish folk songs. However, musically he was mainly influenced by the German romantic composers such as Weber and Beethoven and he developed a classical music style which owed more to what was happening in Germany, rather than his Scottish inheritance. In 1829 he met his younger contemporary Felix Mendelssohn, during the latter's visit to Scotland. Mendelssohn admired his work and encouraged him to visit Germany to study, writing a letter of introduction for the Scotsman to take to his family.

"The bearer of this letter is a young man who has shown me much kindness here... I earnestly beg of you to smooth down for him as much as possible any difficulties he may encounter in Berlin... He is very fond of music; I know a pretty trio of his composition and some vocal pieces that please me very well..."

John Thomson picture courtesy
University of Edinburgh Fine Art Collection.

Thomson spent sometime in Berlin and seems to have made a good impression on Mendelssohn's family. Fanny Mendelssohn, herself a talented musician, described him as the man "whom I like best among all the Englishmen (sic) I know," and the two of them swapped musical compositions. He went on to meet Schumann and study with Ignaz Moscheles a friend of Beethoven, in Berlin and Leipzig. He also seems to have visited Paris in 1830.

His musical works included three operas "Hermann", "The House of Aspen" and "The Shadow on the Wall" which were performed in London, a fine bagatelle, a rondo and other pieces for piano, two piano trios, a flute concerto and a flute quartet, concert arias and a six part glee "When Whispering Winds". His "Drei Lieder" of 1838, a copy of which he dedicated to Mendelssohn, are considered to be comparable with Schumann's famous songs composed two years later. He also edited the "Vocal Melodies of Scotland".

In October 1839 he was appointed the first ever Reid Professor of Music at Edinburgh University. A few months after this he married Janet, daughter of Dr John Lee the Principal of the University. In February 1841 he celebrated the first Reid concert, which also included programme notes - possibly the first example of what has now become standard practice in concert programmes. However, his career was cut short by his death from heart failure in May 1841. He was just 35 years old.

Information courtesy O. Drake

Kelso Bridge and its Connections

Built 1803

Kelso Bridge is seen by architects, engineers and historians as something very special, for it was in its day a pioneering design.

For most of Kelso's history the river Tweed was a major barrier which had to be crossed by ford or ferry. There had long ago been a bridge linking Kelso to the royal burgh of Roxburgh but it was destroyed in the wars of the Middle Ages. When a bridge was built at Kelso in 1754, it was the only bridge between Berwick and Peebles, so it was a great asset to the town. Its collapse during an October flood in 1797 was therefore a shattering blow and a replacement was urgently sought.

KELSO BRIDGE, in ROXBURGHSHIRE. &c

Published according to Act of Parliament, by Alex.' Hogg, N.º 16, Paternoster Row.

Kelso Old Bridge, picture courtesy of Kelso Archive.

John Rennie from East Lothian, one of the out-standing civil engineers of his day, was commissioned to draw up the design. He executed public works all over Britain and Ireland, for example the Kennet and Avon canal, harbours such as Dunleary, Berwick and Newhaven, naval docks, the new naval arsenal at Pembroke, the Plymouth breakwater and many bridges including Waterloo bridge in London. Rennie was said *"to make bridges that for beauty surpass all others and for strength seem destined to last to the latest posterity."* His design for Kelso included, for the first time in Britain, the use of the semi-elliptical arch. This allowed for the creation of a level roadway resting on five arches, each with a span of 73 feet. Its polished stone was supported by handsome columns and pilasters. Work began in 1799 with the construction of coffer dams below the site of the old bridge, where the bedrock would provide secure foundations, and the bridge was completed by 1803.

A government loan of £15,000 was secured to pay for Kelso Bridge with the money to be paid back by raising tolls. The toll house can still be seen at the town end of the bridge and the groove worn in the parapet by the thousands of pennies scraped along it by reluctant toll payers. The new bridge ensured that Kelso prospered, especially after the arrival of the railway made it a vital link to the station at Maxwellheugh. For Queen Victoria's visit a triumphal arch was built at the end of the bridge. However in 1854 Kelso

was the scene of dramatic riots when local people, realising that the tolls raised had already paid the cost of the bridge, demonstrated for several nights. After the army was called in the riots died out - as did the tolls soon after. Rennie's Bridge has continued to serve the town well. Designed to carry horse and cart, it coped with the arrival of 40 tonne lorries, eased by the opening of the Hunter Bridge in 1997.

Rennie continued to develop the ideas he had used at Kelso in London and elsewhere. Most notably London Bridge, designed by Rennie, though completed by his son George in 1831, used the same design he had pioneered at Kelso. In 1968 this bridge was sold by the City of London Council to an American Robert P. McCulloch for $2,460,000. It was taken apart and transported to Lake Havasu City, Arizona, where it was carefully reconstructed. Rennie's London Bridge based on Kelso Bridge has become Arizona's second biggest tourist attraction after the Grand Canyon.

Kelso Bridge

The proudest moment of a Kelso Laddie's year in office is the colour bussing when he is presented with the town flag. It is preceded with the following words. The same words which have inspired this Homecoming project.

"In Peacetime and wartime men from Kelso have gone out to the four corners of the world in pursuit of their duty, and we symbolise our recognition of their deeds by our Kelso Laddie dipping the Town Flag to the North, South, East and West of Kelso Square."

At each of these points a Lady Busser will tie a Blue or White Ribbon to the Standard. These four Ribbons bear one word each, Freedom, Honour, Valour and Wisdom".

Kelso Laddies have contributed to the world in many ways:

Military Service

Kelso Laddies served in all 3 of the armed services. The 1962 Kelso Laddie Angus Balden was the last Kelso Laddie called up for National Service.

Several served during the Second World War with the first Kelso Laddie Bobby Service serving in the desert campaign. Wat Landels was with the Parachute regiments that landed in Normandy, Wat bumped into local Butcher George Hap Wilson during the campaign but was captured later that day, he managed to escape a week later and return to his unit. Rodger Fish was a Captain in ENSA.

Sport

Many of the Kelso Laddies have represented Kelso and their country.

In rugby, 1976 Kelso Laddie Eric Paxton gained Scottish caps against Ireland and Australia and was renowned world wide on the Sevens field winning many Borders Medals especially Melrose. He also played at the Hong Kong Sevens on several occasions reaching the Final in 1982 with the Scottish Border Club. He reached the semis in 1983 when the side lost to Fiji. 1959 Kelso Laddie Arthur Hastie, was the manager of the 1983 Scottish Border team in Hong Kong, and as an SRU member went on to manage the Scottish team which won the last 5 Nations Tournament. Arthur also managed a Scottish select to Zimbabwe and Scottish tours to Australia and South Africa.

1975 Laddie George Hinnigan coached Kelso Harlequins for several years and during that time they were voted the best youth team in Britain after winning the Scottish Youth Cup.

Migration

It has to be said that the majority of Ex Laddies still stay and work in Kelso in the Scottish Borders. Sandy Charters was one of the first to emigrate to the then named Rhodesia to run a tobacco farm. Bobby Service also spent time in Africa but returned to live in Yetholm. Neil Cowe has emigrated to Australia.

Picture Scotsman Publications

Kelsae Bonnie Kelsae

There's a fine auld toon in the Borderland,
By the sides o' the banks o' Tweed,
Where the salmon leap on the silver strand,
And the game and the cattle feed.

There are beauties rare in that lovely scene,
In the valley o' the Tweed,
And she sits right there, as the Border Queen,
Mid the hill and the vale and the mead.

Her days of strife and war are gone,
Now the Border Feuds are past,
Yet our Kelso's sons we will praise anon,
And their fame shall for ever last.

Then let us all with heart and voice,
Sing the praise of Kelso's name,
We will work and play, and aye rejoice,
That "Kelsae is oor Hame".

List of Kelso Laddies

Year	Name	Year	Name
1937	RW Service	1977	Colin Dumma
1938	Rodger Fish Jnr	1978	George Halliday
1939	David W. Clow	1979	Derek Wichary
1946	Alex. Charters	1980	Colin Henderson
1947	Dickson Robb	1981	Neil Hastie
1948	David Brunton	1982	Graham Young
1949	David Gray	1983	Colin Gibson
1950	David Weatherston	1984	David Thomson
1951	Adam Fairbairn	1985	Scott Forbes
1952	Walter Landels	1986	Douglas Veitch
1953	John Hume	1987	Jim Henderson
1954	Tom Laing	1988	Steven Dickson
1955	George McCombie	1989	Douglas Harvey
1956	Bert Nicholson	1990	Derek Lauder
1957	James Campbell	1991	Keith Riddell
1958	Peter Halley	1992	Graham Sweenie
1959	Arthur Hastie	1993	Michael Ballantyne
1960	Norman Hume	1994	Neil Cowe
1961	Jimmy Simpson	1995	Chris Gillie
1962	Angus Balden	1996	Steven Scott
1963	Kenneth Ballantyne	1997	David Stewart
1964	Alastair C Neil	1998	Craig Scott
1965	George Swanston	1999	David McKay
1966	Tom Fairley	2000	Darren Paxton
1967	Len Stevenson	2001	No Kelso Laddie
1968	Jim Hogarth	2002	Scott McKenzie
1969	Ian Cleghorn	2003	Mark Halliday
1970	Dennis Poloczek	2004	Ross Glendinning
1971	James Hinnigan	2005	Kevin Wilson
1972	Derek Hall	2006	Andrew Haig
1973	Michael Tait	2007	Gareth Ford
1974	Gordon Little	2008	Adrian Gajczak
1975	George Hinnigan	2009	Robert Hogarth
1976	Eric Paxton		

Ken Smith

A formidable back row forward, G. K. Smith made his Scotland debut in 1957 against Ireland and went on to win 18 caps for his country up to 1961, beating Wales, Ireland, France and Australia, but only ever managing a draw in the Calcutta Cup and coming close without winning against South Africa.

A Borders farmer he was called up for the 1959 British and Irish Lions tour to Australia and New Zealand and played in 16 games on tour – only three less than the tour captain Ronnie Dawson. He started four of the six Test matches, scored a try against Australia on top of two, in the first match of the tour against Victoria and another in New Zealand, before succumbing with his fellow Lions to the mighty boot of legendary All Black Don Clarke. That Lions team was famously hailed as the 'Buccaneers' for its ambitious attacking style and was generally felt not to have earned a just reward in losing three Tests from four in New Zealand in an overall record of 27 wins in 33 matches. Smith was the first of what are now five Kelso players to be selected for the Lions and he went on to become president of the Scottish Rugby Union and chairman of the International Rugby Board.

Roger Baird

Gavin Roger Todd Baird was born in 1960 in Kelso, but, like his fellow Kelso internationalist John Jeffrey later, he was educated at the popular rugby-playing Merchiston Castle School.

Baird was a 'flyer' on the rugby field - one of the quickest and most clinical of players ever to pull on the Kelso and Scotland jersey. While still at

Merchiston, he played scrum-half for the Scottish Schools and also for the full Kelso Sevens team, collecting a Melrose winners medal at 17.

He made his debut for Scotland in a memorable 24-15 victory over Australia at Murrayfield on 19 December, 1981, and it provided a taste of what was to come. Roger made another 15 consecutive appearances on the left wing for Scotland which culminated in only the second-ever Grand Slam achieved by Scotland, in 1984.

It was an astonishing run that yielded eight Test wins, including Scotland's first in the southern hemisphere, against the Wallabies in Brisbane in 1982, first back-to-back wins ever in Cardiff, two wins and a draw in three Calcutta Cup clashes, and a famous 25-25 draw with New Zealand at Murrayfield in November, 1983, which helped to lay the foundations for the wonderful 1984 clean sweep of the Grand Slam.

The Kelso man went on to win 27 full Test caps in all, with the most bizarre statistic being the fact that he failed to score a single try. It was bizarre because Baird scored in virtually every arena in which he played - be it schools rugby, youth, 1st XV club level, sevens and was even one of the stars of the British and Irish Lions tour to New Zealand in 1983, where he scored six tries in 11 appearances against some of the best wingers in the world.

He was a great creator, a player opponents feared giving space to, yet still he often came close to scoring for Scotland. But on numerous occasions his desire for victory ensured he gave a final pass to make sure of the try and the Scotland win when he could have selfishly gone for the line and touched down himself. He played in the centre for Scotland against England and brought the curtain down on his international career against Ireland in 1988.

John Jeffrey

John Jeffrey will forever be remembered as a key figure in Scotland's Grand Slam triumph of 1990 – only the third such success by Scotland in over 100 years of competing. However, there was much more about the Kelso farmer which made him a familiar and popular figure in world rugby. Purely in a rugby sense, Jeffrey was held in high esteem by

teammates and opponents alike due to his hardness on the field of play, which, combined with his innate rugby ability, pace off the mark and handling skills, made him one of the most talented flankers of his generation.

Dubbed 'The White Shark' by the media because of his distinctive blonde hair – still to this day, when he appears at games in France, they shout 'shark' when he passes – "JJ" was capped 40 times by Scotland between 1984 and 1991 and his break from the back of the scrum against England at Murrayfield in 1990 was the catalyst for the match-winning try.

He was also a British and Irish Lion in the 1989 Tour of Australia, when the Lions schedule had been trimmed to just 12 matches, all hosted by Australia, and the Lions went on to win the series by two Tests to one.

Alan Tait

Born in Kelso in 1964, Alan Tait left the area at the age of four when his father (also Alan) accepted the offer of a career in Rugby League with Workington. For the next 13 years, Alan learned the 13-a-side game until his father retired and the family returned to Kelso.

With everyone at Kelso High School preferring 15 men on the field, Tait

had to adapt to the union code. He did so successfully, becoming part of Kelso's Division One Championship-winning team and then replacing John Rutherford in Scotland's very first Rugby World Cup match, with France in Christchurch in 1987.

Tait played in eight consecutive Tests, but then followed in his father's footsteps and turned to rugby league, firstly with Widnes and then Leeds. He reached the pinnacle of the game, appearing in Premiership and Challenge Cup Finals, winning the Harry Sunderland Trophy for Man of the Match twice – and won 16 caps for Great Britain.

Tait returned to union with Newcastle at the onset of professionalism in the 15-a-side code, and won the English Premiership, returned to the Scotland team and won 19 more caps. He helped the British & Irish Lions team to victory in South Africa – only the second ever win there in 100 years – and Scotland to the last Five Nations Championship in 1999, with tries against England and France. He retired after the 1999 World Cup as one of Scotland's most prolific try-scorers, and has since coached the Borders, Scotland and Newcastle.

Ross Ford

Ross Ford joined the brethren of British and Irish Lions in 2009 when he was a late call-up to Ian McGeechan's tour to South Africa.

Ross was a popular head boy at Kelso High School, and played for Kelso Harlequins (u18s) before making his debut for the full Kelso 1st XV. Then, he was a back row

forward, and also captained Scotland U16 and represented his country at U18, U19 and U21 levels. Ross in 2001 was the youngest sportsperson to be selected for the Scottish Institute of Sport.

In 2002, Ross was selected for Scotlands Commonwealth Games Sevens squad in Manchester. Playing as a flanker for the now disbanded Border Reivers, head coach Tony Gilbert saw his potential and moved him to the hooker position. He repaid their faith by swiftly turning into a great front row player and won his first senior cap for Scotland in 2004 – his debut jersey hangs in his old primary school, Edenside, on Inch Road - and he made his first Six Nations Championship appearance in 2007.

Ford became the first choice hooker in Scotland's Rugby World Cup 2007 squad, scoring his first try for Scotland in his first World Cup appearance, against Portugal, and this year toured South Africa with the British & Irish Lions. On 4th July 2009, Ross gained his first British and Irish Lions Test cap when he came on as a substitute to play his part in the successful 28-9 victory over the Springboks.

The year of the Homecoming 2009 is a celebration of the 250th anniversary of the birth of Robert Burns, Scotland's national bard. In this board we consider the episodes in Burns life that linked to Kelso and district.

The Kelso Piper

John Anderson my Jo is founded on an old song set to an air which is said to have been a piece of sacred music previous to the Reformation. In James Johnson's *Scots Musical Museum* it is claimed that the hero of the song is John Anderson – the town piper of Kelso.

"John Anderson, my jo, John,
When we were first acquent;
Your locks were like the raven,
Your bonie brow was brent;
But now your brow is beld, John,
Your locks are like the snaw;
But blessings on your frosty pow,
John Anderson, my jo.

John Anderson, my jo, John,
We clamb the hill thegither;
And mony a cantie day, John,
We've had wi' ane anither:
Now we maun totter down, John,
And hand in hand we'll go,
And sleep thegither at the foot,
John Anderson, my jo"

Robert Burns

Burns' Border Tour

Burns' Border tour of 1787 is well documented by local Burns historian Archie MacArthur making use of Burns journals of the time. Burns says of Kelso

"Breakfast at Kelso – charming situation of Kelso. Fine bridge over the Tweed enchanting views and prospects on both sides of the river particularly on the Scottish side"

This was washed away at the end of the 1700's. The buttress now sticks out of the St Andrew's church garden. Burns recorded details of his visit. "Introduced to Mr Scott of the Royal Bank, charming fellow. Dine with the farmers club – all gentlemen talking of high matters each of them keeps a hunter from £30 to £50 in value and attends the fox hunts in the country"

Burns was impressed by the turnip and sheep husbandry and commented that the soil was superior to Ayrshire. He dined with a Mr McDowal at Caverton Mill and also dined with Sir Robert Don who he described as

"A pretty clever fellow but nothing in him - far, far from being a match for his divine lady"

His lady was Lady Harriet Don, sister of the Earl of Glencairn, a staunch supporter of Burns who had backed earlier editions of his books. Then Burns also notes "the beauty of the ruins of the old monastic house, The Friars at Friarshaugh", a site commemorated now in Kelso Civic Week Whipmans Ride.

The James Thomson Connection

The Earl of Buchan invited the poet to be present at the coronation of Thomson's bust at Ednam. As he could not attend he sent a laurel wreath and wrote the poem "Address to the Shade of Thomson."

It was as well that he did not attend as the company of the evening became rowdy and the bust was smashed before it could be crowned. The revellers on the evening having to place the laurel wreath on a book of poems rather than the bust.

Address to the Shade of Thomson

While virgin Spring by Eden's flood,
Unfolds her tender mantle green,
Or pranks the sod in frolic mood,
Or tunes Eolian strains between.

While Summer, with a matron grace,
Retreats to Dryburgh's cooling shade,
Yet oft, delighted, stops to trace
The progress of the spiky blade.

While Autumn, benefactor kind,
By Tweed erects his aged head,
And sees, with self-approving mind,
Each creature on his bounty fed.

While maniac Winter rages o'er
The hills whence classic Yarrow flows,
Rousing the turbid torrent's roar,
Or sweeping, wild, a waste of snows.

So long, sweet Poet of the year!
Shall bloom that wreath thou well hast won;
While Scotia, with exulting tear,
Proclaims that Thomson was her son.

Robert Burns

Connecting the Kelsos

Kelso people have gone throughout the world and some of them have named the place they have settled after their home town.

Kelso, Washington, U.S.A.
Founded by Peter Crawford from Kelso, Scottish Borders, in 1884. Educated as a surveyor and civil engineer at the University of Edinburgh as well as in London and Southampton, he emigrated to America in 1843 to join his brother, Alexander. He came west in 1847 and kept a journal of the trip overland by wagon train. He staked a claim on 240 acres at the mouth of the Cowlitz River.

Margaret Riddell at Kelso, Washington

Kelso, Minnesota, U.S.A.
KELSO Township, settled in 1855-56 and organized in 1858, bears a name that was originally given by A. P. Walker, a surveyor, in 1854 or 1855, which "is of Scotch derivation," being the name of a town on the Tweed River in Southern Scotland.

Kelso River Minnesota

Kelso, Ontario, Canada
Kelso Conservation area is on the site of a farm founded by Adam Alexander from Scotland.

Kelso Lake, Ontario

Kelso's Twin Town – Orchies, France
The connection began in 1980 when Kelso High School and the College de Pevele of Orchies started a pupil exchange. This led to the formal twinning of the two towns in 1987. During subsequent years many people from Kelso and Orchies formed lasting friendships.

Orchies Town Hall picture Christine Henderson

Kelso, Scotland

Other Kelsos around the world that we have discovered

Kelso	Arkansas	Kelso	Nebraska
Kelso	California	Kelso	North Dakota
Kelso	Idaho	Kelso	Oklahoma
Kelso	Indiana	Kelso	Oregon
Kelso	Kansas	Kelso	Queensland
Kelso	Michigan	Kelso	Tasmania
Kelso	Mississippi	Kelso	Tennessee
Kelso	Missouri	Kelso	Virginia

Kelso, South Africa
Named after Kelso in Scotland by Henry Cooke.

Kelso, New South Wales Australia
Kelso, New South Wales Australia is a suburb of Bathurst, in the Bathurst Regional Council area. It is the original European settlement in the area, the first farmers took up grants here in 1816. It was named after Kelso, Scotland by Thomas Brisbane for his wife who was born there.

Kelso Village
BOOK 1
By Adan McRae and Carol Churches.
To celebrate the Centenary of Federation 2001

Kelso, New Zealand
Named after Kelso the home town of one of the town's first settlers, James Logan. Kelso was subject to frequent flooding and in 1980 the settlement was relocated. Nothing much now remains except this cairn.

Photographs Ken Nichol

Kelso War Memorial

World War One excluding Gallipoli

First name	Surname	Year of death	Country
William	Affleck	1917	France
John	Aitchison	1915	France
William	Aitchison	1918	Italy
Robert	Alexander	1916	France
Robert	Allan	1918	France
Alfred	Anderson	1917	Scotland
George	Anderson	1917	Belgium
Henry	Anderson	1917	France
Andrew	Armstrong	1917	France
Peter	Armstrong	1915	France
Thomas	Biggar MM	1918	France
James	Black	1917	France
William	Black	1918	France
James	Boyle	1917	France
James	Brannan	1918	France
William	Brockie	1917	Israel
James	Brown	1917	France
James	Brownlie	1915	Belgium

First name	Surname	Year of death	Country
Robert	Bruce	1917	France
James	Brunton	1915	Egypt
John	Brunton	1917	Belgium
Gavin	Buchanan	1915	France
Alexander	Buddo	1918	France
John	Burton	1917	Israel
William	Callander	1917	Israel
Peter	Campbell	1917	France
H R	Stanley-Clarke	1916	France
Ralph	Coulter	1917	Israel
Alexander	Cowans	1917	Israel
James	Craig	1917	Israel
George	Crerar	1915	France
Robert	Croall	1918	Scotland
John G G	Cuthbert	1916	France
Simon	Dalgleish	1917	Israel
James	Dickson	1917	Israel
Thomas	Dickson	1918	France

First name	Surname	Year of death	Country
George	Dodds	1916	Scotland
Thomas	Donaldson	1917	France
Andrew	Douglas	1918	France
John R	Douglas	1918	France
Thomas	Douglas	1916	France
Walter	Douglas	1918	France
William	Douglas	1917	Belgium
Adam	Dumma	1917	Belgium
John	Dumma	1915	Scotland
Andrew	Dunn	1918	France
William G	Ewart	1918	France
John	Fairbairn	1918	France
Thomas	Fairbairn	1915	France
James	Fairgrieve	1915	Turkey
Hugh	Ferguson	1917	Egypt
Alexander	Forbes	1915	Turkey
Walter	Forrest M.C.	1917	Israel
Andrew	Fortune	1917	France

First name	Surname	Year of death	Country
James	Fox	1917	France
John H	Fox	1917	France
Thomas L	Fox	1915	Belgium
William	Fox	1917	Belgium
James	Frater	1917	Belgium
Thomas	Galbraith	1917	France
William A	Galbraith	1917	Israel
William R	Galbraith	1917	France
William A	Galloway	1917	France
James	Gardiner	1917	Belgium
John D	Gibson	1916	France
William H	Gillis	1918	France
James	Gilroy	1918	France
John	Gleed	1918	France
John	Grahamslaw	1915	Turkey
John	Guthrie	1918	Scotland
Peter	Haig	1918	France
William	Haig	1918	Belgium

First name	Surname	Year of death	Country
George A D	Hall	1916	France
James	Hall	1919	Germany
Walter H	Halliday	1916	Belgium
Walter Heriot	Halliday	1917	Belgium
William	Halliday	1918	Belgium
Adam	Handiside	1917	France
John	Hanvey	1915	Turkey
Walter C	Henderson	1918	France
Alexander	Hendry	1916	France
John	Hewitson	1918	France
Andrew J	Hogarth	1917	Scotland
Henry	Hogarth	1915	France
John A	Hogarth	1917	France
John S	Hogarth	1917	France
George	Hope	1917	Israel
James	Hope	1916	France
William	Hume	1915	France
Andrew	Inglis	1917	France

First name	Surname	Year of death	Country
Andrew	Jack	1918	Belgium
Bertie	Jackson MM	1916	France
Percival H	Jackson	1915	Belgium
Henry E	Johnston	1916	France
Andrew	Kerr	1915	France
Andrew	Kerr	1919	France
Arthur D	Kerss	1918	France
George R	Kinghorn	1917	France
J Leslie	Laidlaw	1916	France
William	Leishman	1918	France
Alexander W	Lillico	1917	France
Alexander	Lindores	1917	Israel
William	Lockie	1914	France
Arthur D	Luke	1917	France
George	Luke	1915	France
David	Lunam	1918	France
Thomas	Lunham	1915	Egypt
Patrick	Lynch	1915	Turkey

Kelso War Memorial

World War One excluding Gallipoli

First name	Surname	Year of death	Country
Alexander	Mabon (Kelso)	1919	Scotland
Alexander	Mabon (Roxburgh)	1915	Turkey
Robert	Mabon	1918	France
Thomas	Mabon	1918	France
Frank C	Mack	1920	Scotland
John	Mack	1918	France
Francis J	Mein	1916	Scotland
James D L	Melrose	1918	Belgium
William A	Milne	1916	France
Gilbert	Moffatt	1919	Scotland
David	Morris	1918	India
George	Murray	1917	Belgium
Alexander	McBain	1918	France
Alexander	McCraw	1917	France
James	McCraw	1915	France
William	McCraw	1917	France
Alex A	McDonald	1916	France

First name	Surname	Year of death	Country
Robert B	McGeorge	1919	Scotland
George	McGregor	1917	France
John	McKenzie	1918	France
James	McLaren	1917	France
William S	McLaren	1917	France
Horace	McLeod	1916	India
John	McRobb	1917	Belgium
John J	Neillans	1915	France
Richard J	Newton	1915	France
James	Patterson	1917	France
John H	Patterson	1917	France
Robert M	Patterson	1914	France
Robert	Patterson	1917	Greece
Thomas	Patterson	1916	France
William	Paulin	1918	France
Andrew	Pringle	1919	France
William	Pringle	1918	Scotland
Joseph M	Quarry	1915	Malta

First name	Surname	Year of death	Country
James	Queenan M M	1918	France
George	Raeburn	1918	France
George G	Raeburn	1918	Belgium
Charles	Reid	1916	France
George	Reid	1916	France
Horatius	Reid	1919	Scotland
Peter J	Reid	1915	Turkey
Edward J P	Roger	1918	Belgium
James	Rodgers	1917	France
Andrew	Robertson	1918	France
George D	Robertson	1915	France
John I	Robertson	1917	France
John	Robertson (Eckford)	1918	France
William	Robertson	1916	Belgium
William	Ruddiman	1915	France
John	Rutherford	1917	France
David	Sanderson	1918	France

First name	Surname	Year of death	Country
David	Scott	1917	Belgium
George	Scott	1917	France
James F	Scott	1918	Scotland
James	Service	1915	Scotland
John	Sharpe	1915	France
Robert	Sinclair	1915	France
Frank W	Smail	1915	England
Ian S	Smith	1918	France
William F	Somervail D.S.O. M.C.	1918	France
Walter	Stavert	1916	France
Archibald G	Steel	1917	France
Thomas	Steel	1917	Belgium
William M	Steel	1917	France
John C	Stormonth - Darling D.S.O.	1916	France
James	Swanston	1916	France
Mark	Tait M.M.	1918	France
Charles	Thomson	1917	France

First name	Surname	Year of death	Country
James T	Thomson	1917	Egypt
John	Thomson	1917	Egypt
George	Tice	1917	France
John	Tice	1917	Belgium
William	Tice	1918	France
Andrew	Tinlin	1916	France
James	Titilah	1917	France
George W	Turnbull	1918	France
James	Turnbull	1917	Israel
William	Turnbull	1915	Turkey
Andrew	Turner	1916	France
James	Turner	1917	France
Thomas	Waddell	1915	France
James	Watson	1915	France
Robert	Watson	1917	Belgium
Thomas	Watson	1916	France
George	Weir	1916	France
Alexander F	Whitelaw	1916	Belgium

First name	Surname	Year of death	Country
George H	Whitelaw	1917	France
George T	Whittle	1918	France
John	Wight	1918	Belgium
Adam W	Wilson	1918	Belgium
Charles	Wilson	1916	France
Thomas	Wilson	1918	France
William	Wilson	1915	France
Francis M	Wood	1915	Greece
James	Wright	1915	Turkey
William	Yeomans	1917	Israel
Christopher	Young	1917	Egypt
James	Young (Kelso)	1918	France
James	Young (Makerstoun)	1918	France
Thomas A	Young	1917	France
Thomas J B	Young	1918	France

Kelso War Memorial

Gallipoli - 12th July 1915

Rank	First name	Surname	Regiment	Cemetery
Pte	John	Ballantyne	KOSB	Helles Memorial
Pte	William	Barnett	KOSB	Helles Memorial
Lieut	Andrew	Bulman	KOSB	Helles Memorial
Pte	George	Cairns	KOSB	Helles Memorial
Pte	Frederick K	Callander	KOSB	Helles Memorial
Pte	John	Darrie	KOSB	Helles Memorial
Pte	George	Davidson	KOSB	Helles Memorial
Pte	Alexander	Drummond	KOSB	Helles Memorial
Pte	Richard	Eckford	KOSB	Helles Memorial
Pte	Alexander	Fair	KOSB	Helles Memorial
Pte	Andrew J	Gray	KOSB	Helles Memorial
Pte	John	Hardy	KOSB	Helles Memorial
Piper	Andrew	Hendry	KOSB	Helles Memorial
Pte	William	Herkes	KOSB	Helles Memorial
Pte	Andrew	Hogarth	KOSB	Redoubt Cemetery
Pte	James	Kennedy	KOSB	Helles Memorial
Piper	James	Kerr	KOSB	Helles Memorial

"In peacetime and wartime men and women from Kelso have gone out to the four corners of the world in pursuit of their duty"

Rank	First name	Surname	Regiment	Cemetery
Pte	William	Mack	KOSB	Helles Memorial
Pte	Walter D	Mair	Royal Scots	Lancashire Landing Cemetery
Pte	James H	Mather	KOSB	Helles Memorial
Sgt	Andrew J	Middlemas	KOSB	Helles Memorial
Corpl	John R	Murray	KOSB	Helles Memorial
Cpl	William K	Neil	KOSB	Helles Memorial
Pte	John	Richardson	KOSB	Skew Bridge Cemetery
Pte	William	Richley	KOSB	Helles Memorial
Pte	John	Robertson (Linton)	KOSB	Helles Memorial
Pte	James	Sanderson	KOSB	Helles Memorial
Pte	Robert	Stavert	KOSB	Helles Memorial
Pte	Charles	Street	KOSB	Helles Memorial
Pte	Baddon T	Walllace	KOSB	Lancashire Landing Cemetery
Pte	Joseph	Wilson	KOSB	Helles Memorial
Pte	Robert	Wilson	KOSB	Helles Memorial
Pte	Robert	Yeomans	KOSB	Helles Memorial

Kelso War Memorial

Rank	First name	Surname	Date of death	Country
Sgt Pilot	Adam	Anderson	21.04.1943	Denmark
Cadet	Hamish	Bews	06.12.1943	Scotland
Sgt Observer	Francis	Boles	17.08.1943	France
Captain	James W	Crawford	05.05.1942	India
Pilot Officer	Stuart S	Campbell C.G.M.	07.09.1944	Malta
Sgt Air Gunner	Robert J	Charters	30.01.1944	England
Pte	Archibald N	Cockburn	18.11.1942	Egypt
L.A.C.W.	Flora A	Childs	17.05.1945	Scotland
Lieut	William F	Donaldson	24.01.1945	Netherlands
Stoker	Thomas S	Donaldson	17.01.1942	England
L/Corpl	James	Douglas	04.02.1945	Scotland
L/Corpl	Andrew	Easton	12.10.1943	Algeria
L/Corpl	Alexander	Gibb	18.11.1940	Scotland
Sgt	Clifford	Hawker	11.05.1940	India
Gunner	John C	Hogarth	03.12.1942	Tunisia
Stoker	Douglas	Irvine	03.08.1940	England
Pte	James	Ker	18.11.1940	Scotland
Pte	George J	Leitch	31.05.1940	France
Radio Officer	Ian	Lyle	30.01.1941	England
Sgt Air Gunner	Alexander	Lyle	27.07.1942	Germany
W O Navigator	Allan A W	Melrose	28.06.1944	Belgium

> *"In peacetime and wartime men and women from Kelso have gone out to the four corners of the world in pursuit of their duty"*

Rank	First name	Surname	Date of death	Country
Sgt W O Air Gunner	William P	Morrison	17.06.1943	Scotland
Stoker	James	Muir	03.11.1942	England
Pte	Robert T	Murray	19.11.1940	Scotland
Sapper	John B	Murray	21.06.1946	Indonesia
C.P.O.	Walter	Patterson	02.03.1942	England
Sgt. Rear Gunner	William	Pratt	15.08.1944	Poland
Driver	Alfred C	Richardson	16.06.1945	Malaysia
L/Corpl	James M C	Piercy	28.03.1943	Burma
Corporal	Alexander B	Raeburn	14.10.1944	Netherlands
Pte	James	Robertson	02.08.1943	Sicily
Major	John	Stormonth - Darling D.F.C.	01.08.1945	Italy
3rd Engineer	Thomas J	Sear	15.01.1942	England
Pte	Colin	Stewart	18.06.1940	France
Guardsman	William	Thomson	06.06.1944	Italy
Pte	George D	Tait	31.05.1940	Belgium
Pte	Robert	Turnbull	01.07.1943	Italy
Pilot Officer	Charles R H	Underwood	28.07.1942	Egypt
Sgt Air Gunner	Thomas B	Utterston	26.11.1944	Netherlands
Pte	John	Veitch	13.09.1943	Italy
2nd Lieut	Andrew M	Watson	10.08.1943	Scotland
Gunner	Andrew	Weatherston	19.03.1941	Scotland

Quiz

1. The Emperor of which country gave James Brunlees the Order of the Rose?
2. John Robson won Commonwealth Bronze in which Canadian city?
3. Where did Alistair Moffat's "Walking the Line" end?
4. Thomas Brisbane built an observatory in which Australian city?
5. Where did Sir Walter Scott's grandfather Robert farm?
6. Georgiana Solomon was a lady principal in which South African city?
7. William Glass settled on which island in the South Atlantic?
8. Shedden died in which South American country?
9. Where did Horatius Bonar write many of his hymns on camel back?
10. In which country did W. H. Ogilvie learn his droving skills?
11. Before returning to Kelso James Dickson was a merchant in which city?
12. From where was the final version of Lyte's "Abide with me" sent home?
13. At which famous bowl did Thora Ker make a solo guest appearance?
14. Forrest made his rods with greenheart wood from which continent?
15. Peter Crawford founded a new Kelso in which American state?
16. Where did Sir George Henry Scott Douglas buy The Vampire?
17. Fans from which country still shout "shark" at John Jeffrey?
18. Jack Ker captured the wickets of which country's top 3 batsmen?
19. Rosemary Payne reached the final in 1972 at which Olympics?
20. In which country did Ross Ford score his first World Cup try for Scotland?
21. Where did Wat Landels land with the Parachute Regiment?
22. Where was William Edgar Tait partner in a timber business?
23. Mr la Noski visited James Roberton to learn farming from where?
24. James Thomson who wrote the words to "Rule Britannia" is buried where?
25. Where was Thomas Stoddart's wife from?
26. Where did Ian Hastie become Far East Armed Forces light heavy weight champ?
27. Thomas Pringle helped lay a foundation stone in which South African town?
28. Where in Germany did Jane Stoddart learn German and teach?
29. In which building did William Jerdan apprehend the assassin of PM Percival?
30. Where were 33 Kelso men killed on 12th July 1915?
31. George Taylor travelled from Kelso to where?
32. Sir William Purves was Chairman of which Royal Jockey Club?
33. In which Canadian province can you find the Kelso Conservation area?
34. Where was London Bridge (based on Kelso Bridge) reconstructed?
35. In 2004 Mathew Pinsent won his fourth consecutive Olympic Gold at which games?
36. Where did Burns's "Summer with a matron grace" retreat to?
37. In which country did Mendelssohn invite John Thomson to study?
38. In 1824 William Fairbairn erected two waterwheels in which European city?
39. The Ballantyne's moved their printing business from Kelso to where?
40. Where did Mary Lundie Duncan help during a cholera epidemic?